SECOND SIGHT

SECOND SIGHT

A Miraculous Story of Vision Regained

Charlotte Sanford
and Lester David

M. Evans and Company, Inc.
New York

Library of Congress Cataloging in Publication Data

Sanford, Charlotte, 1936-
  Second sight.

  1. Sanford, Charlotte, 1936-   2. Presbyterians—
United States—Biography.   3. Blind—Biography.
I. David, Lester, joint author.   II. Title.
BX9225.S278A36   285′.1′0924   [B]   79-10282
ISBN 0-87131-287-5

M. Evans and Company, Inc.
216 East 49 Street
New York, New York 10017

Manufactured in the United States of America

9 8 7 6 5 4 3 2 1

To Jesus Christ and His love,
which I have experienced through a devoted family
and wonderful friends,
and to my three children—
Stephanie, Julia, and Pete.

Prologue

This is the story of an incredible event that occurred to me on a hot July day in the small Midwestern city where I have lived all my life. Blind for fifteen years, I opened my eyes and saw the beauty of a rose, I saw my doctor's face, and I saw my three children.

It is the story of the despair that had gripped me when the events of my life seemed overwhelming and I came, quite literally, within an inch of ending it.

It is the story of love and human weakness.

But most of all, it is a story of faith that I want to share with all who are troubled, who are finding it difficult to cope with an ever more complex world, who are handicapped in any way.

In St. Matthew (17:20), we read:

"If ye have faith as a grain of mustard seed, ye shall say unto this mountain, Remove hence to yonder place, and it shall remove. . . ." The love of Jesus and the power of the Holy Spirit moved my mountain, which came close—so very close—to crushing me.

· Here is the true story of how it all happened.

Chapter One

One morning early in May, when I was nearly three years old, I wandered out into the backyard of Grandma Akers's little farmhouse and sat cross-legged in front of a patch of larkspur. The blue of the five petals on each flower was so intense, the yellow centers and slender green stems so vivid that I stared entranced until my mother called me inside for lunch.

As far back as I can remember, colors, smells, and the touch of things were extraordinarily keen to me. Most young children, I know, enjoy poking and picking at the wonderful world they discover every new day of their lives, but my feel of the world enlarging before me was somehow different: sharper, clearer, more detailed.

When I stroked velvet, I could almost feel every soft strand of the low dense pile. Silk was incredibly smooth beneath my fingertips and denim unusually harsh and coarse. On nice days, the Kansas sky was always a marvelous blue which edged into a darker color toward the horizon. My white starched dresses were always dazzling; the red checks on a tablecloth fairly leaped out at me; and even the blackness of a stove, just plain black to most people, was lustrous to me.

On Grandma's farm there was a reddish-brown cow whose milk was always strained through the tea towels. After Grandma boiled the towels and hung them out on the line, I would go out, touch them, and put my nose to them. The scent was so pure and clean that even now I can close my eyes and remember it. Food cooking on the stove or heaped on my plate smelled exceptionally delicious, or, if I didn't like it, exceptionally horrible! When I stretched full length on the ground under the huge weeping willow in the backyard, where the grass never grew, and buried my face in the ground, I could smell the sweet pungency of the earth itself.

Sounds were also sharper to my ears. Noises would startle me excessively, even though others would not consider them especially loud. I could detect—actually hear—music in rainfall. I would lie in bed at night or sit beside a window during the day and listen for a long time to the harmonies of falling raindrops, rain that other people would consider a nuisance. Even now, when the house is quiet, I can listen to the rain and hear its melodies.

Doctors cannot explain why my senses were so finely tuned so early in my life, but I will be bold enough to offer my own answer. It is important that I say this at the very beginning because it is the foundation stone upon which my story rests.

Many years of darkness lay ahead for me, years during which my sight was blotted out and I could no longer see the blueness of the sky or the green of the grass or a rainbow's reflection in a puddle after a shower. I believe, and looking back has reinforced rather than weakened that belief, that God was preparing me for what was to happen only too soon in my life. I can offer no proof, of course. Scientists, I know, demand the evidence of documentation; I have none except my strong belief. I also believe that God was preparing me in still other ways.

The Interurban, a bus that ran on tracks, squealed to a halt on the highway. Dad, Mom, and I got off; brown hair flying, I skipped down the narrow country road several hundred feet to the farm which Grandma and Grandpa Akers owned on the western edge of town.

I bolted into the house and to the kitchen which was as tiny as Grandma herself. Only four feet nine inches tall, she had everything scaled down to her size. The cabinets were so low that even I could reach them, though I was barely six; the work space seemed as though it was made for a rather large doll, and even the stove had stubby little legs.

Grandma Opal Akers, her silver hair framing her tiny features and her clear eyes dancing, hugged me with her small arms and asked if I had brought along Dad and Mom. "Of course, Grandma," I answered seriously, and in a moment, they stepped through the door.

Little wonder I looked forward with such undisguised eagerness to our visits to the farm. I was an only child; my father worked for an oil refinery, and on his pay, we managed to scrape by, but barely. We lived in a three-room apartment in Coffeyville, a small city which sits astride Route 166 in the southeastern corner of Kansas, just north of the Oklahoma border. The closest large city is Tulsa, about 80 miles south. Coffeyville is a growing community now, but it is still small-town America. Our latest telephone book, which includes the neighboring town of Dearing, is only 64 pages long.

Coffeyville may be just a tiny dot on the map for most people, but we think it's an old and pretty famous place. The seat of Montgomery County, it was founded by Col. James A. Coffey in 1869, who established a trading post here. The development of natural gas and oil fields in the region at the turn of the century helped the town prosper. And it had some famous (and infamous) citizens at one time and another. Wendell L. Willkie, the Republican candidate for President against Franklin D. Roosevelt in 1940, once taught school here. In 1892, the three Dalton brothers and two other desperadoes tried to rob the town's two banks simultaneously, but angry citizens engaged in a 30-minute shoot-out with them, killing two of the brothers and two members of their gang. Four townspeople died

11

in the gunfight. The whole story is memorialized in the Dalton Museum on East Eighth Street.

Our little family was cramped into an apartment on the first floor of a large house on Eighth Street. In the tenements of large cities, it would be called a railroad flat; all the rooms were in a straight line, a front or living room, a bathroom off a little hall, the little bedroom, and finally the kitchen at the back.

My father was Charles Howard Kenneth Akers, if you please, but nobody but Mother ever called him anything but Pete. I doubt whether he would have turned around if anyone called out his full name. He was born and raised on a farm in Jefferson, Kansas, a town so small you can't find it on any map—it was hardly more than a few stores and a stop on the Interurban. Dad lived on the farm until, at the age of eighteen, he married my mother, who was a year older, and moved into town. They had been childhood sweethearts. I was born March 17, 1936, in Low's Clinic, a very small hospital in Coffeyville.

Our entire family would gather at the farm for Thanksgiving and Christmas dinners, or on Sundays, for Opal and Will Akers were generous, warm-hearted people who loved to be surrounded by family. On cold days, when the sharp Kansas winds coming off the prairie nipped our noses, we would all squeeze into the little gleaming white dining room, where extra leaves stretched the table until it almost touched both walls. At one end, nearly dwarfed by its height, sat Grandma Opal, and Grandpa Will sat at the other. In between, beaming and laughing, were Emma and Donald Johnson, my other grandparents; Opal's sister Blanche and her husband Jim; and my dad's three brothers and their wives, Uncle Dwight and Aunt Pauline, Uncle Harry and Aunt Zerita, and Uncle Milton, who was a bachelor; and Aunt Rubye, my mother's sister. Besides me, the only other child was my cousin Dick, a year and a half older, who was Dwight and Pauline's son.

12

Who could forget the huge Thanksgiving turkey, so beautifully browned and fragrant, which Grandpa Akers proudly and skillfully carved? Or the huge platters of fried chicken accompanied by great mounds of snowy mashed potatoes with yellow rivulets of home-churned butter and the dark specks of pepper that gave them such a distinctive mellow-sharp taste? After dinner, there was always a special dish: my own. Grandma, busy and bustling as she was, would let me concoct something of my own, desserts of peaches and nuts, with a tower of whipped cream (I shudder now at the calories!), and others like it. Grandma would bring my efforts to the table as though they were her own, and everyone would taste, smack their lips, gaze skyward, and say it was the best he or she had ever tasted, not looking at me, of course, though everybody knew who made it. Naturally, I would be beside myself with joy.

The dining room window looked out on the pasture where, in the summer, a long table was set up for picnics. Again, there were those great mounds of chicken and potatoes, or sometimes a huge roast beef, and heaps of brilliant green peas, bowls of spicy gravies, warm bread and rolls snatched right from the oven, preserves, homemade of course, and crisp green salads and heavenly puddings, and vast amounts of ice-cold milk from the cow who, tail swishing the flies away, stood watching us.

And Christmas! Kansas winters are usually mild, but sometimes a white blanket of snow covered the prairie as we chugged out to the farm on the Interurban. Soon I was enveloped in the warmth and coziness of the little house, and I remember staring awestruck at the huge Christmas tree in Grandma Akers's living room, a balsam fir Grandpa had cut himself. Grandma loved blue; the carpeting in the living room was blue, and the drapes on the windows were blue. The tree, too, was trimmed mostly in blue—blue tinsel strung round and round it in a spiral, blue ornaments in all shapes hung from its branches. And, of course, it shone brilliantly with dozens of little blue bulbs.

I spoke of other ways I was being made ready to withstand the shocks.

One involved the inner me, that mysterious labyrinth of the mind and spirit, which was being firmed up, layer by layer, in my early years. A sense of security, of self-esteem, of worthiness as a human being, were being bred into me. Not that this inner core wouldn't be tested to the utmost! There would be times of despair, times when I felt unable to carry on—indeed, times when I nearly gave up. But that inner shield held.

Where it came from is no mystery to me. In these days when moral standards are changing with bewildering speed and even the basic unit of our civilization, the family, is being threatened, I feel it is crucial to make this point crystal clear to everyone who reads this book.

Families are losing their influence upon their children; too many are disintegrating, their members flying off in all directions. As a result, young people are growing up with warped values that lead them into all sorts of troubles.

Nobody has the final answer to the question of which traits are inherited and which are acquired through the influence of the home, the neighborhood, friends, in other words, the environment. But experts in human behavior have come to a conclusion that cannot be doubted: that many personal characteristics are *contagious*. Thus if an individual has his grandfather's surly, ungovernable temper, he or she has most likely learned it from the grandfather. If the same person has a pleasant, sunny, giving disposition, the probability is great that he or she learned it at home. If he is weak and frightened of the world, *that* was communicated at home. If he is strong, the strength was absorbed from the strength of a mother and a father.

I know—and I know this with a conviction that bores to the very marrow of my being—that the strength to endure the harsh, brutal blows that lay ahead came from the love and trust of my parents and those frequent gatherings of the

14

entire family in that small house and on those few acres of Kansas prairie land. I emerged from this crucible able to face life and all its harsh realities.

Somehow, even though a great deal of my early strengthening came from my own home, the farm wraps it all up for me because it stands for the united family, all of us together, loving each other and giving by guidance, by example, and by love the vital confidence one small girl was to need so desperately to cope with adversity.

Another strengthening factor, the most important of all by far, was infused into me by my family.

My family was not aggressively religious. Neither Mom nor Dad, nor anyone else, had ever shaken a finger under my nose and threatened to call down God's vengeance upon my head if I did not behave! No, they all had what I like to call a quiet faith, and like still water, it ran deep.

A turning point came when I was eight, which made me embrace God fully and for all time.

Grandma Emma and Grandpa Donald Johnson, my mother's parents, lived in a corner house on Tenth Street, a few blocks from our apartment. It was gold-colored and had a wide old-fashioned front porch.

Two years after the United States entered World War II, my dad was drafted into the service, and despite the family allotment we received from the government, it was hard making ends meet. So Grandma and Grandpa asked Mother and me to move into the big house with them. Mother got a job as a cashier in a restaurant and had to work nights and on Sundays.

Grandpa Johnson, who also worked at the oil refinery, was a short, stocky man with iron-gray hair. Gifted with a beautiful tenor voice, he would launch into song at the drop of a hat—or even the sight of a cereal box. One morning at breakfast Grandpa did just that. He picked up a packet of cold cereal on the back of which were the words of "Beautiful Dreamer," Stephen Foster's lovely song. As

Grandma bustled around the kitchen, Grandpa, true to form, a spoonful of cereal suspended in midair between plate and mouth, began singing the words. I joined in, of course, and as the last words died away, we burst into laughter and resumed our breakfast.

He was a member of a quartet that sang wherever anyone asked them, or just for the fun of it. The members would come to the house regularly for practice sessions. Grouped around the old upright piano in the living room, they would sing through their repertoire, which ranged from hymns such as "The Old Rugged Cross" and "In the Garden" to country ballads and Stephen Foster songs.

Meanwhile, their wives would be seated around the large gas circulator stove which was plunked squarely in the middle of the living room and do their embroidery. Of course, I would always manage to be there someplace, peeking over the shoulders of the ladies as their needles flashed in the intricate workmanship or moving over to Grandpa's side as the quartet sang. Afterward, there would be tea and cookies, and when the singers and their wives left, the three of us (Mom had to work at the grill room) would group around the radio and listen to "The Eddie Cantor Hour," "Lux Radio Theatre," "Green Hornet," "A Date with Judy," and other shows.

Grandma Johnson was a chubby little woman with a beautiful face and lovely blue eyes that had more than a hint of sadness in them. I never learned why. Every person is entitled to little pockets of personal privacy, and Grandma Johnson had hers. A generous, full-hearted human being, she gave me something I could not touch, feel, smell, eat, or wear but which was the greatest gift one human can bestow upon another.

One Sunday morning in late fall, while Mother was at work and Dad was still in the army, I went to church with both my grandparents. It was the United Brethren, a small red-brick building on the corner of Eighth Street, with room for only 50 worshippers, all working people who sat on its plain wooden pews. The floor was uncarpeted, the planking beneath our feet squeaked protestingly, and the cold wind seeped through the ill-fitting window sashes and any crevice it could find. We sat bundled in our coats. Grandpa sang in the choir, and I, sitting next to Grandma, slipped my hand into her warm, soft one.

The minister called upon the worshippers to sing the hymn, "Living for Jesus." As the small organ struck the introductory chord, I happened to turn and look at Grandma Johnson. Her round face was lifted, and the sadness had left her bright blue eyes. I can think of no other word to describe that face other than that it shone, shone with a light I had not observed before, an effulgence that came from somewhere within. I watched entranced as she sang about living her life to please Him in everything she did.

Her radiant face had an amazing effect upon me. I knew, though I was barely eight, that she meant every word, and silently in my heart I said: "If this is what living for You means, Jesus, if this is the kind of lady that kind of life produces, then this is exactly what I want to do too. Because I can see You in her, Jesus. I can see You!"

At that moment, just as the hymn ended, Grandma Johnson, who was still holding my hand, squeezed it just a little, and I returned the pressure. No, I don't think she ever knew what had happened to me. And I never told her. But from that moment, I gave my life to Jesus.

I had not had much opportunity to learn about faith. Dad was still in the army and Mother seemed to be working all the time. I knew that I had undergone a powerful emotional experience that was to alter my life, give it meaning and direction. Giving my life to Jesus meant that I had made a conscious personal commitment to Him, that young as I was I had experienced a spiritual encounter all by myself, in a personal way, while sitting in a small brick church gazing at my grandmother's rapt face as she sang to the glory of God.

I was only a third-grader when this great experience happened to me. A few weeks later, I fell ill. My sickness could have been the beginnings that were to test my newly-found faith to the utmost.

Chapter Two

When I was only two months old, an epidemic of scarlet fever swept through Coffeyville. Parents of young children were terrified because in those days there were no penicillin or sulfa drugs to vanquish the killer germs that invaded the ears, noses, and throats of its victims. A shockingly high number of children, especially under five years old, were dying.

Mom and Dad took every precaution to keep me out of public places and, of course, made certain no child came within yards of me. Nonetheless, one morning in late May —I had been born the previous March—a rash popped out on my neck, chest, and back. Within hours, the tiny red spots began spreading all over my body, and sure enough, I had a fever. Mother telephoned the doctor who arrived within the hour.

He looked at me, saw the telltale signs, and told Mother: "I'm very sorry to say that it's scarlet fever." My dad had been called at work, and he rushed in just in time to hear the diagnosis. Mom told me later she was terrified because her sister had contracted the disease in Missouri one year and almost died.

The house was quarantined, and my parents kept long vigils by my bedside. They had been told to summon the doctor at once if they noticed any unusual signs. Gradually the rash faded, and as I was told later, I didn't seem to have a sore throat or even much of a fever after the first day or two. It looked as though I was making an uneventful recovery.

But Mother had noticed something strange.

One morning when she came into the bedroom, she saw that I had moved my head around and seemed to be staring at the light bulbs in the ceiling. Gently she turned me away, but wherever she put me, I twisted my head so that I could stare at the light. Mother also noticed that one of my eyes had become red and puffy, and that it was matted with some sticky substance.

She telephoned the doctor. He, too, noticed that I was looking fixedly at the light. He examined my inflamed eye, instructed Mother to wash it gently with a solution of boric acid, and watch it. He could offer no explanation as to why I kept twisting and turning to stare at the light.

I know now that the complications that can follow scarlet fever can include damage to the ears, kidneys, heart, and, in some rare instances, the eyes.

I recovered in a few weeks. Much later, I would tell this story to the dozens of doctors I was to visit. "Was this," I asked, "where it all began?" Some said, "Maybe"; none could say for sure. But Mother and I share the strong belief that everything that was to happen in later years started that summer before I was three months old.

I sprouted like a weed, looking something like a little crane with my long skinny legs. We had no kindergartens in Coffeyville, and the years couldn't pass fast enough so that I could enter first grade and march to school like all the bigger children on the block.

In the spring before that important first-day-of-school, I was lying on the floor on my stomach, a crayon in my fist and a coloring book spread out in front of me. Mom, watching me from an easy chair where she was sewing, saw me brush my eyes with my free hand.

"What's the matter, dear?" she asked. "Caught something in your eye?"

"No," I replied. "Least I don't think so."

"Then what are you doing?"

"Nothing. Just trying to get these black spots away."

"What black spots?"

"*These* black spots!" I answered a little impatiently, rubbing my eyes with one hand and pointing with the other, as though Mother could see them as plainly as I.

Mother, who recalls the precise conversation, frowned and came over to me. She studied the coloring book, looked to see if some dust or perhaps insects were somewhere around, and, seeing nothing, became a little concerned, though certainly not alarmed. Nevertheless, she decided to take me to an eye doctor who dropped medication into each eye to dilate the pupils and peered into them through an intricate instrument—an ophthalmoscope, I learned later. Finally he said it wasn't anything unusual; many people, he explained, had the sensation of seeing spots or so-called vitreous "floaters" before one or both of the eyes. Behind the lens of the eye, the doctor told Mother, is a large space filled with vitreous humor, a jelly-like substance, tiny specks of which move about. Actually, the doctor said, floaters were much more common in adults than in children, but in any case they usually don't mean anything.

In 1944, Dad came home from Camp Hood on furlough prior to being shipped to the Pacific. And just a few days after he arrived my throat became sore, my tongue took on a strawberry hue, and I felt just awful. Mother recognized the symptoms: I probably had scarlet fever again. The doctor confirmed it, and I was put to bed. This time I was the only kid in town with the disease.

I lay in bed, utterly miserable, until the illness ran its course. Dad, all six feet two of him, pin-neat in his uniform, hovered over me constantly. His hair was still a light brown, and there was a smile on his oblong face, but his brown eyes were hurting. Dad always suffered when I did.

I was about nine when a stab of pain that made me wince shot through my eye and into my head. It started in

21

the left one, which soon became angrily red and puffy; in a few days, the inflammation spread to the right eye.

Mother took me to several doctors, all of whom shone bright lights into my eyes and peered into them with their intricate scopes, but none could discover anything wrong. Soon, however, the pains and inflammation subsided, and I forgot about them.

But a few months later there was another lancing pain, again beginning in the left eye and causing both eyes to swell and redden. The flare-ups continued at irregular periods as I grew older.

By 1946, Dad had been discharged from the service. Now began our round of visits to specialists to find out what was the matter. Mom and Dad took me to Joplin, Missouri, Tulsa, Oklahoma, Wichita and Kansas City, Kansas, and perhaps a dozen other large and small cities. Every time they heard of a new eye specialist they would call for an appointment, pack up, and leave with me in tow.

Always there were lengthy examinations and explanations that differed widely, but no clear-cut answer. Several doctors reported that I had an eye infection, which was certainly true. Others saw floating particles, and one doctor told my parents to rush me back home and have my tonsils removed at once because they were, he said, "spilling poisons all over her body." Those were the years when infected tonsils were being blamed for everything from colds to heart disease and were being yanked out by the hundreds of thousands every year. Since then, medical science appears to have changed its views, and nowadays, tonsils are not considered the archvillains they once were. (One old-fashioned doctor, talking about a report that unnecessary operations, particularly hysterectomies, were being performed these days, commented, and I suspect he was only half joking: "We got all the tonsils, now we're starting on the uteruses.")

When Mother and Dad heard the warnings about poisons, they rushed me back to Coffeyville, and almost before

I knew what was happening, I was in bed contentedly eating ice cream to soothe my sore throat, my tonsils gone.

But the flare-ups continued.

By this time my sight began to fade, but so slowly that I noticed nothing. Words in my school books seemed blurry to me, I couldn't make out the features of people sitting across the table, and on the street, homes and trees and cars blended together in a hazy surrealistic background. Grass, even from a short distance, looked like a lovely carpet of green, highlighted by darts of sunsplashings as though painted by an impressionist; I could not make out individual grass blades.

I didn't think it at all strange. After all, wasn't this the way things were supposed to look? I was like the men and women whose hearing gradually becomes impaired in later life. Without being aware of what is really happening, they become unable to hear high tones, such as bells and whistles, begin to misunderstand conversation, and grumble about people who don't "speak up," and keep turning up the volume of the television, complaining that the words aren't clear. In exactly the same way, my world was becoming shadowy—but wasn't everybody's?

During this time I had vision tests, of course, and was fitted with glasses. The doctors had told my parents I was myopic, or near-sighted, but myopia occurs with many children. Despite my slowly fading vision, I was easily able to pass the quickie eye tests given to us at school.

My school work did not suffer at all; in fact, my grades were better than average. Nobody knew that I listened very carefully to what the teachers were saying and was memorizing the lessons instead of studying them in the books I gradually became unable to read.

God is good to young people. He doesn't give the vast majority of them the most predominant emotion of our age—anxiety. That comes later. And so as a child I hardly worried about my growing affliction; in fact, I don't remember looking upon it as a handicap at all.

My chief concern as I went through grade school and in junior high was perfecting the art of faking so that nobody would notice my failing sight.

I never let on to my friends because, understandably enough, I didn't want to be different.

Memorizing lessons was just one trick I used. I became an absolute master at getting out of things—athletics, for example. I really loved sports, but because I simply couldn't see a ball coming toward me, I knew I'd look an utter fool on an athletic field, so I invented the most elaborate excuses to avoid playing. I had to do something for my parents. Or I had a sore knee. Or I had my—well, you know—and the girls understood.

I remember in the ninth grade we were making a dress in sewing class. I began to fall hopelessly behind because I was unable to thread the needle. I'd always pretend to be terribly busy with something or other as I, with studied carelessness, would ask Joyce Chowning, my best friend, to thread my needle for me. I'd never tell her why and, looking back, I can see her look of resignation as though saying: "How lazy can a person *be?*"

In English class, we would take turns reading paragraphs of a poem or selection from a classic. Quickly I would count the number of students ahead of me, then move my fingers down to the paragraph I would be called upon to read. Slowly, laboriously, I would read it to myself over and over, so that by the time my turn came, I had practically memorized it, and neither the teacher nor anybody else suspected.

Boys were becoming an interest as I came into adolescence.

Dances and parties were pretty much of a cinch to the expert in fakery I had become. In junior high, about eight or ten girls would occasionally chip in a total of $10 or $15— allowance and baby-sitting earnings for the most part—and rent Moose Lodge, the fraternal organization headquarters, which had a roomy dance floor.

None of us would have dates. We'd hand out invitations in school to the boys, and then hope we'd be asked onto the dance floor.

I made some goofs; one in particular was a doozy. I slipped an invitation into the hand of the school bully none of the girls could stand. I mistook him for someone else with the same height and build. He took it and came to the dance. When he arrived, I heard gasps.

"Who in the world asked *him?*" one of the girls asked. "Yes," I replied heatedly, "who'd be dumb enough to invite *him?*" As soon as the words came out, I realized who the dumb one was. I kept my mouth shut and hoped for the best, but it wasn't such a great party.

The lights at the dances were always turned low, so that made bluffing easier. Still, many times I'd mistake one boy for another or, what was worse, not even see if anyone was coming over to ask me to dance.

Once a boy tapped me on the shoulder. "Look," he said, "if you don't want to dance, say so straight out. But don't turn away like some kind of prima donna just as I'm opening my mouth." That's exactly what I did to the class president.

"Oh, no," I said with a straight face, thinking fast. "I felt a sneeze coming on and I didn't want . . ." "Oh," he said, mollified. "In that case . . ." I got out of that one okay.

After that, I peered a lot closer into the gloom to see if anyone was coming over to me. When I noticed a shadow looming out of the darkness, I'd make some kind of flip crack to a girlfriend. "Look who's coming. Robert Taylor, I'm sure." If the ploy worked, my friend would reply: "Sorry, Charlotte, it's only Jim." Or, Hank, or whoever. If it didn't, I took my chances. To be on the safe side, I'd never call a boy by name until I was reasonably certain I knew who he was.

Joyce Chowning, as short as I was tall and skinny, became my best friend. We made lists of boys; Joyce did the writing because I would pretend to have a sprained finger.

We would number them by our preferences. I remember that a boy named Jim Logan turned up on several of our lists. Joyce told me confidentially: "Now, Charlotte, don't you get to like him. You see, he . . ." And then she'd proceed to give me a long list of things that were wrong with Jim Logan. Of course, after that I was turned off, although I had really started to like Jim and was all ready to honor him by putting him at the head of my list.

What I *didn't* know, and should have suspected, was that Joyce secretly had a wild crush on Jim; she ended up becoming Mrs. Jimmie Dale Logan and having five lovely children. She is still my best friend and has remained so during the years.

My acute sense of touch was an invaluable aid in helping me fake the decorating of parties. Once Joyce and I festooned our garage for a big affair. Dad's fortunes had improved, and we had moved from our railroad flat to a frame house on West First Street. For the first time we had a living room, dining room, three big bedrooms, a lovely large kitchen, and a double garage. In the backyard there was room enough for a garden!

Joyce and I decided to have a Hallowe'en party they'd talk about for a long time. We rushed around gathering real corn stalks, bales of hay, pumpkins, sheaves of wheat, apples, and everything else that went with the occasion. To this day, I can't understand how I did it. I picked up a basketball and thought it was a pumpkin, but quickly recognized it before anybody saw. I must have hammered my fingers until they were raw, trying to get the decorations in place. Somehow, though, it all turned out happily, and no one was yet the wiser.

But it all started to close in on me fast, and not even my most skillful efforts at bluffing could hide the fact that my sight was going.

Mother discovered it for the first time one afternoon after school, when I was thirteen. I had come home, dropped my books, and sauntered over to the piano. I had carefully placed the piece on which I was working atop the other selections so that I wouldn't have to rummage through the pile and perhaps pick the wrong one. I opened it on the piano ledge and peered at the notes.

All I could see was a blur of black and gray. I leaned closer, and some of the notes separated from the haze that clouded them. I played them, but they seemed to recede and again become part of the fuzzy lines running across the sheet. Once more they popped out, only to tease me again and disappear.

Frustrated, I banged the keys with both fists and blurted: "Darn it all! I can't see the notes!"

Mother, knitting in an armchair at the other end of the room, looked up sharply.

"What do you mean, dear?" she asked quietly, but with a sharp edge of worry in her voice.

I was beyond caring. Something told me my faking days were over.

"Just what I said, Mom," I answered irritably. "These notes. I can't make them out. They're all blurring together."

Mom came over to the piano, hoping to find a badly printed page, she told me later. But the practice piece I was working on was sharp and clear.

I asked Mother to put into words what happened next:

That's when your father and I really became upset (she wrote). We talked it over that night after you were asleep. We now knew something was terribly wrong, and I shivered a little in bed, although the night was not especially cold. Your father said he'd leave no stone unturned to find out what's happening.

Next day, a neighbor told me about a young eye

specialist who had just arrived in town. We called him, and even though it was his usual day off, he agreed to see you. The examination took a long, long time, and after it was over, he sat with Daddy and me in his office and—at last—gave us a diagnosis.

Dr. Morse explained that you had a condition known as iritis, which is an acute inflammation of the colored portion of the eye. You had all the symptoms—pain which radiated to the temples; edema, or an accumulation of fluid, in the upper lids; a blurring of vision; a dull and swollen iris, and a pupil which was irregular in shape instead of being normally round.

Dr. Morse was kind but frank.

He told us that the disease was still largely a mystery to medical science, that doctors did not know for sure what brought it on, and that treatments with atropine drops or ointment could help. The recently discovered drug cortisone could control the recurring bouts of inflammation, he said, but he admitted that so far no actual cure had been discovered.

Deep inside our minds, Daddy and I must have known what he was trying to tell us, but can anyone blame us if we were like ostriches, hiding our heads in the sand, refusing to face the scary thought?

Dr. Morse would leave no stone unturned. He sent us to a colleague in Kansas City, and together they agreed that you should go to the famous medical center in Rochester, Minnesota, the Mayo Clinic.

We did not hesitate. We packed at once and set off for Parsons, not far from Coffeyville, where we caught the train to Rochester. I prayed silently that maybe, just maybe someone there might tell us how to stop this terrible thing that was happening.

Although it was March, the sun was shining brightly, and we decided only at the last minute to take winter overcoats, though what on earth we would need them for in this glorious weather was beyond me.

28

Well, that fine weather lasted until the train crossed the Iowa border. Then the wind picked up, and snow began to fall. By the time we neared Iowa City, we were in the middle of a near-blizzard. I whispered thanks to God that He had sent us the message to take our heavy coats. The train slowed to a crawl, then began inching ahead through the heavy snow. Finally, it stopped completely.

For 19 hours, the train was stalled on the track. Thank God, the fuel had not run out, so it was reasonably warm inside, but there was no diner and nothing whatever to eat. The toilets were stopped up and the stench from them was just awful.

But the worst part was that we were almost out of the cortisone tablets the doctor had prescribed for the inflammation. Cortisone is a steroid hormone secreted by the outer part or cortex of the body's adrenal glands which lie near the upper end of each kidney. Synthetic steroid compounds are now manufactured as medications which have been found to be extremely useful in the treatment of dozens of diseases, especially those involving inflammation. It was still brand-new—the doctor told us it had only been discovered in 1949—and cost a dollar a tablet. That's pretty expensive even today; you can imagine what it was back then. We had enough to last us from the time we left Coffeyville until our arrival at the Mayo Clinic.

The train sat there in the blinding snow, lurching forward a few feet, then moving back. Your father looked at you, curled up on the seat with your hand over your eyes. There was only one tablet left. Without the cortisone, the inflammation would get worse, and the pain would be agonizing.

He leaped to his feet, and ran down the aisles of the cars until he found the conductor. Quickly, he explained the emergency, and together they left the train and talked to a highway patrolman who was alongside the tracks. Through the snow, he and the officer went in search of those precious—and very scarce—tablets. They drove for miles until they found a pharmacy that carried them. Before the druggist would sell him some, he telephoned Coffeyville to verify the prescription.

In a couple of hours, your father was back on the train, holding three more cortisone tablets.

Thankfully, they kept you comfortable until, a day late, the train finally arrived in Rochester.

I remember that week at Mayo as though it all happened yesterday.

We had found rooms in one of the boarding houses not far from the clinic. My appointment had been rescheduled for that Tuesday morning. We all got up at 6 A.M. and, bundled up against the bitter cold, walked down the street to a restaurant for breakfast. The snow had been cleared from the sidewalks, but on the curb it was as high as Dad's head—and he was six feet two!

Feeling sickish, my eyes hurting, I managed to swallow some eggs and hot cocoa and then went with my parents to the admitting office where we signed in and waited until my number was called. By this time, the three of us had grown accustomed to sitting and waiting in doctors' offices. I daydreamed and dozed as the time passed.

Finally my name was called, and I went inside.

I had been admitted as an outpatient, which meant that I would come to the clinic at eight each morning and leave about six in the afternoon.

We remained in Rochester an entire week, during which I underwent all sorts of tests, from blood examinations to x-rays of the skull, and answered what seemed to me to be hundreds of questions asked by a number of doctors. It was the most thorough physical examination I had ever undergone. What would it show?

Chapter Three

One week after our return, Dr. Morse sent for me. Mother and I went at once to his office. He held a two-page letter in his hand.

"I have the report from the Mayo Clinic," he said. He patted my hand and said in a soft voice:

"You have what doctors call posterior uveitis, a rare eye disease, which has been going now for a number of years. Frankly, we don't know very much about it. It's related to iritis, but I have to tell you that it's more severe.

"Now listen carefully, Charlotte," he began. "Picture an eye in your mind. It's got a dozen or so parts," he said. "The white part, which is called the sclera, is a tough, fibrous coating that protects the entire eyeball. The colored part in front is the iris, and the black center is the pupil. The pupil adjusts for light, like the lens of a camera. When it's dark, the pupil automatically opens to admit more light; when it's bright and sunny, the opening gets smaller. Got it so far?" I nodded.

"In front of the pupil," he went on, "is a rounded part called the cornea, and behind the pupil and iris is the lens. On the rear of the eyeball is the retina, which contains many cells that are sensitive to light.

"Now here's how a person sees: When somebody looks, let's say, at a tree, the light goes through the lens which does the focusing—that is, makes the tree sharp and clear. It contains many small muscles that change the shape of the lens automatically to make the proper adjustments. Next, the image hits the retina which in an instant converts the light energy into nerve energy. This nerve energy is caught by nerve cells which transmit the image to the optic nerve behind the eyeball, and this, in turn, sends the image to the brain. And so a person sees the tree.

"But let's go back.

"Beneath the sclera, or outer coat, is another coat called the choroid which covers the back part of the eyeball. This contains lots of blood vessels that nourish the various parts of the eye.

"And attached to the lens is a ring of muscular tissue called the ciliary body which does the job of focusing I told you about.

"These three parts, the iris, choroid, and ciliary body, make up what we call the uvea.

"And that, Charlotte, is where your trouble lies."

I concentrated carefully on his words.

"Now in posterior uveitis, which is what you've got," Dr. Morse went on, "both the choroid and the overlying retina become inflamed. As the disease progresses, the eyes can become badly damaged because of the inflammation, causing the formation of lots of scar tissue in the vital parts of the eye, and a good deal of degeneration of the eyes as well.

"Unfortunately," Dr. Morse continued, "we don't know what causes your uveitis, or anyone else's. All those tests you had at the Mayo Clinic—remember them?—were made on the possibility that some clue might be uncovered. Maybe you had a hidden infection somewhere that was the source of all your trouble. But everything checked out fine.

"So all we can say now is that you've got a disease of unknown origin and that we're going to do our best to treat it and help you."

Well, so finally we knew.

Knew everything but one fact that Dr. Morse mercifully kept from me. The final paragraph of the Mayo Clinic report stated that the outlook for me was "not good."

Dr. Morse did all he could to combat the infection and stop the relentless degeneration of the vital parts of my eyes. He even tried a centuries-old technique, called fever therapy, which was used in China, Japan, and, oddly enough, by the Indians of our state. The Indians would throw water over stones heated in hot fires to create a primitive version of a steam bath, into which they would place a sick individual. The idea was to raise the body's temperature high enough to conquer the disease.

"Fever," Dr. Morse explained, "increases the number of white blood cells in the body, and that increase can play an important role in defending the body against the invasion of bacteria. In a very real sense, a variety of white cells called leukocytes move through the blood vessels, hunting down and destroying disease-causing germs. They can squeeze through even the tiniest openings in the capillary walls, corner the germs, and just engulf them. Now we know there is an infection somewhere in your eyes, but so far we haven't been able to root it out. Let's try this."

These days, fever therapy has almost entirely been supplanted by antibiotic drugs, but in the late 1940s and early 50s, it was still used on occasion. I was admitted to the hospital where I was the central character of a little drama. The doctors would induce a high fever by injecting me with a foreign substance. They tried typhoid germs but could only get my fever as high as 103. Oddly enough, the most successful substance was boiled milk, which really heated me up. Every 24 hours, I'd get some of this injected into my bottom, and I'd be watched with eagle-eyed care by the nurses. As soon as my temperature soared to 105, they'd let it remain there for just a couple of minutes, then swiftly douse me with ice and cold water to bring it down, regardless what time of day or night it was. If they left me burning like that for too long, the high temperatures could damage the brain.

It was exciting all right, but unfortunately it didn't work.

My eyes worsened. Once, Dr. Morse took me to Kansas City to be examined by specialists from all over the world who gathered at the University of Kansas Medical Center for conferences. Nobody could solve the problem.

When I was sixteen, a Kansas City doctor reported that the retina of one of my eyes was becoming detached. This is a dangerous condition in which the retina separates from the choroid. Unless re-adhered at once by an electric needle, retinal detachment can cause permanent, irreversible blindness. (Now, one quick zap from a laser beam can literally reseal the retina.)

When Mother heard that, her hand flew to her mouth and, beneath her fingers, I could see her lips moving in prayer. She and the doctor agreed it would be wise to return to the Mayo Clinic for a reexamination.

While Mother and the doctor were discussing the new trip, I rose silently, left the office, and walked down the corridor. I stood for a moment in front of a window in the hall and suddenly the full realization of what lay ahead swept over me for the first time. With the optimism that always resides in children, I had not believed that anything really dreadful would happen to me. But I was sixteen now, old enough to look reality full in the face. And what I saw was a terribleness beyond anything I had ever known or thought.

I was going to be blind!

All those trips to doctors in all those cities far from my home, all those interminable examinations, medicines, hospitalizations—nothing was going to help me. The whole world, growing dimmer with every passing week, would soon be blotted out entirely, and I would live the rest of my life in darkness.

With the realization came, at last, the tears. I stood there before that window, looking out at the gray street, my hands at my sides as great sobs racked my body. For long minutes I wept uncontrollably. Thoughts I may have pushed back into the depths of my mind now poured out. What would my future be like? My future no longer lay in dolls or toys or fun and games with the kids, but in the grown-up world. I wasn't going to be like other girls. Would I have a husband of my own, a family? Or work. How could I work? What would I do?

I was alone in the corridor during that climactic moment when the path my life would probably take became only too plain. I remember thinking: Was that prophetic? Would I be alone during all the years to come?

And then, as suddenly as the tears and sobbing came, they stopped.

The great faith in Jesus and the depth of love for Him that had been building within me took hold, just as the slipping brakes on an automobile hurtling downhill might abruptly catch and stop the wheels which are spinning out of control. No, I would not be alone. How could I have forgotten those great words of the Twenty-third Psalm:

Yea, though I walk through the valley of the shadow of death,
I will fear no evil: for thou art with me;
thy rod and thy staff they comfort me.

And these, from Psalm 27:

The Lord is my light and my salvation;
whom shall I fear?
The Lord is the strength of my life;
of whom shall I be afraid?

I walked back into the doctor's office, my tears dried.

Mother and I went home, packed, and in August of 1953 we made our second trip to the Mayo Clinic, where the doctors found no retinal detachment. But my right eye had become shrunken and was totally blind. The left had become worse, though not yet gone. We returned home, prepared to face what had to be faced with strength and dignity. I caught Mom and Dad crying when they didn't think I could notice, but I broke down only once more when a second, and to me an even more devastating, blow came some years later.

I did not know then in what manner God would help. Nobody does. But I did remember that at the age of eight I had given my life to Jesus in trust and in faith, and I had faith and trust that whatever suffering was in store, God would be at my side, for He is the ultimate healer.

Later, in times of discouragement, sorrow, and the blackness of depression that was, in a very real sense, darker than the absence of sight, I would find the ability to endure in a God who reached out for me. There is a passage in the Bible (John 8:12) that helped more than I could possibly say to sustain me:

Then spake Jesus again unto them, saying, I am the light of the world: he that followeth me shall not walk in darkness, but shall have the light of life.

Yet I would not be human and fallible if I didn't question God and wonder: "Why me?" Or if I didn't, then and in later years, feel sorry for myself. I was young, not unattractive, and I wanted what most other young girls would surely have—fun, light-hearted gaiety, and a future.

But I also came to understand that we are all imperfect human beings. Some of us have physical defects, others strive all their lives against personality and emotional handicaps. A great minister (the late Reverend Dr. Harry Emerson Fosdick, founding pastor of the Riverside Church in New York City) once wrote: "Bring on your strong and shining Apollo who never had a handicap, who, with integrated personality, for-

36

tunate circumstance and physical health has lived untroubled by limitations, and however energetic may be his active service in the world, there are some things he cannot do for us that Helen Keller can." Miss Keller, who lost both her sight and her hearing as a result of a serious illness before she was two years old, conquered those overwhelming handicaps and lived a long life during which she became fluent in several languages, wrote many books and articles, lectured all over the world, conducted class discussions, and worked indefatigably with soldiers who were blinded in World War II.

We reached Coffeyville just as dusk was falling. Neither Mom nor I said anything, but the symbolism hardly escaped us.

There would be hard years ahead.

Chapter Four

I've often wondered when the kids first became aware that I couldn't see things as they did. Somewhere along the line they caught on, but nobody said anything. They just *did* things.

For example, when I was in the hospital for the fever therapy, Joyce would come by almost every afternoon as soon as school was out.

"Hi," she greeted me. "I've got a new Cherry Ames. Let's see what she's up to."

The Cherry Ames series was all the rage then among the junior high girls. Joyce would come in and sit down; but instead of offering me the book she would open it and read to me until we were both tired.

During the six weeks I was in the hospital, nobody ever sent me a book. Instead, the kids in school took up a collection and got me a record player and a big batch of records. I thought it was a beautiful thing for them to do, and I listened to it for hours on end.

I got a strong feeling that they were really troubled by what was happening to me. At our age, few of us had had any serious physical problems. I know that they probably sensed that hearing might be my link to the world.

When I got out of the hospital my teachers and principal gave me another great gift—I didn't have to make up any of the work I had missed! I took up just where I left off, and they gave me full credit as though I had been present in school the whole time.

By the time I reached high school I wore glasses with thick powerful lenses, but I saw the world as though I were peering through layers of gauze. I could read for only two or three minutes at a time without getting tired. And I had to hold the book about six inches from my eyes to do even that. At fifteen feet, a huge elm tree appeared to be a shadow. It was almost impossible to distinguish features.

Today, most children with the vision I had then would not be allowed to go to a public school; they would be sent to a school specifically set up to educate children with eye problems.

However, I continued on to Field Kindley High School. I could not read. I could not make out what was written on the blackboard. I could barely see well enough to navigate the halls on my own.

After classes, my teachers would take the time to print in very large letters what they had written on the board so that I could take it home where I could study by myself or with help.

My tests were given to me orally after regular class. If I had reading to do, the teacher would allow Joyce and me to go out into the hall, and Joyce would read the assignment aloud.

Most of the time Joyce and I would finish early, and we would sit and talk. We were close friends and, to this day, have a beautiful relationship.

At home, my parents would read to me. Fortunately, in those days, we weren't expected to do too much homework. I listened very hard and concentrated on remembering what I heard. So I was able to do pretty well and received mostly A's and B's.

Of course, it wasn't all study in high school. I wanted to take part in many things, and I did.

I always loved singing. I'm a mezzo-soprano and, for a time, took private voice lessons. In school, I was among the members of Robed Choir, the top choir in high school, and I was one of the twelve who was selected for the Madrigal Group. As the best singers in high school, the Madrigals went to contests all over the state, and even though I was terribly nervous, it was a great thrill to represent our school. We loved it.

We were rated on our vocal performance in high school, and I was elated when I received a *One* as a senior, the only girl to achieve this of 150 in my voice range.

One of the big events of the school year was a musical extravaganza called the Kindley Cavalcade, a series of song and dance numbers, sketches, and ballets. Everybody volunteered to do something—whether on stage, or backstage, making scenery and costumes.

When the plans were announced, I was ecstatic because my favorite song, "Deep Purple," was to be the theme for one of the ballets. I talked to Joyce about it.

"I'm going to try out for the ballet," I said. "I'm not sure Mrs. Brooks will pick me, but I'm sure going to try!" Mrs. Emma Jane Staton Brooks, a dance teacher in Coffeyville, was the director of the ballet, and—wonder of wonders—she did select me to be one of the dozen dancers!

Heaven only knows how I made it because I wasn't the most graceful thing in the world. The ballet had a series of movements in which the girls created various steps and platforms.

One of these called for a girl to rise clear to the top of the platforms and dance down the steps in time to the music. It was a little solo and, amazingly enough, I was chosen.

I was elated and petrified at the same time. For weeks we rehearsed endlessly in street clothes and then in purple chiffon dresses that floated as we danced. The first time I moved up the platforms and started down I felt like a circus performer doing a high-wire act while blindfolded. After that, when I discovered I didn't do a headlong dive, it became easier. And at performance time, I came through like a pro.

Nonetheless, I learned later that during the other dances, the other girls would be carefully watching for me. If I would be walking across the stage to reach my starting position, a group of dancers squarely in my path would not run out to grab me or yell after me. They would quickly move out of my way to avoid a collision and, of course, embarrassment.

The cavalcade was an enormous success, and my own sense of accomplishment zoomed sky-high.

Years later, I learned that this was precisely what Mrs. Brooks had in mind when she chose me for that little solo. Now retired and living in Coffeyville, she told me she gave me the part because she did not want me to feel handicapped. "I knew you would work very hard," she said, "and I felt it would help develop your self-confidence." I'll always love her for that.

We had two other very important extracurricular groups in high school. One was the Drum and Bugle Corps and the other was the Tillies, a pep club whose main reason for being was to rouse school spirit for all the athletic games.

Tops was the Drum and Bugle Corps—you were really "in" if you were selected as a member. The corps was an all-girl marching band which performed at all ball games and major school events. Before the games, and in between, the girls would strut onto the field behind the drum major and perform their intricate, snappy routines.

All the girls longed to get into the corps, but only the popular girls, the most beautiful and spirited, were chosen. As far back as I can remember, I had dreamed I would be one of the marchers.

In my junior year, I signed up expectantly. Applicants registered for the Bugle Corps and the Tillies—if you didn't make one, you could get in the other. A high grade average and good moral character were required to stay in either one. Of course, my heart was really set on the Bugle Corps. I didn't make it, but years passed before I learned why.

Mother told me that soon after I applied she and my

41

father were asked to come to school by Harvey Lewis, the teacher in charge of the corps. He was also the director of the choir at the Presbyterian Church where I sang, and he knew me well.

"Mr. Lewis told us he wasn't certain you could see clearly enough," Mother recalled. "He said you had to follow the drum major, watch her fingers carefully, and be able to tell from the number raised which routine was being called."

The school principal, Helen Glosser, the leader of the Tillies, Mr. Lewis, and my parents talked over the situation. They were sympathetic but realistic. Which would be worse —disappointment at missing out on the Bugle Corps or the possible frustrations if I could not keep up with it? In the end, my parents decided I had better not be in the Bugle Corps.

Not being picked hurt a lot. It never even crossed my mind that the reason was I couldn't see well enough. I didn't think about that part. But my folks were thinking ahead. They were level-headed. I would not have been able to do it.

So I joined the Tillies, and for two years, I was vice-president. We went with the teams to all the games and led the cheering. I couldn't do that so I just sat in the stands and cheered. But as vice-president I helped organize pep assemblies, rallies, and pregame bonfires. I arranged for speakers and, when the president was away, conducted the meetings. Once I acted as master of ceremonies at an assembly and had to introduce the speakers and guide the program.

These were things I could do because I could learn them ahead of time and memorize them.

The Tillies also made posters and designed floats for the parades. Dimming vision or no, I did my share of posters, peering at the letters with my eyes practically glued to the oak tag and pinning up the crepe paper and ribbons on the floats. Marching with the Tillies was no problem at all—

I just followed the girl in front of me. Once my guiding star dashed out of line during rehearsal to kick away a rolling ball. I broke into a run after her and nearly wrecked the whole parade, but that was the only mishap I recall.

When I wasn't busy rehearsing for some school or church activity, I went with the other kids to Teen Town, a couple of rooms in Memorial Hall which had been fixed up and set aside for the young folks. It was here I met my first boyfriend and went on my first date. I remember his name, what he wore, what I wore, what he said, what I said, what we did. Everything. A girl's first date is imprinted sharply in her memory, and shadowy vision has nothing whatever to do with the high importance of the occasion.

So Dick Hill came up to me at Teen Town, and after a few days asked me to a dance given by the school's Boys' Club. I accepted, politely, stifling the urge to squeal, "Whee —a date!" that was inside my throat begging to be released. Dick's father took us to the dance in his car and picked us up later. I wore a brown and yellow dress with a high bow in the back that kept opening. On the dance floor, I looked something like a Tillie float with streamers trailing. One of my friends kept racing after me to tie up the bow, but it seemed to have a mind of its own. As soon as she left, it floated free again.

My romance with Dick lasted about as long as any teenager's first crush, which is to say about two weeks. Still, we remained good friends over the years, and we still are. Small-town kids are like that.

There were other dates in high school, but nobody special came along. I loved to dance and sing and have fun, so while I wouldn't say I was the most popular girl in town, I never felt the boys were avoiding me because of my eyes.

About this time I was also very involved in my church work. I taught a Sunday School class of first-graders and was enthralled with them, especially with one little girl named Stephanie. She was a tomboy but was always dressed in starched dresses that billowed about her sturdy legs, matching frilly panties, and ribbons in her hair. One day I went to the supply room for some drawing paper, and when I came back Stephanie was standing on her head showing all the little boys her matching panties.

Years later, I named my first child Stephanie.

My parents were sponsors of a youth group in the church which I joined. They were pretty unusual parents in that they didn't take me to church and drop me; they came right in too. If there were jobs to be done, cakes to be baked, parties and dances to be chaperoned, my parents were the first to volunteer. They were always there to support me in anything I wanted to do or anything that needed to be done. The kids loved my dad. His personality was such that he was always able to relate to and understand the kids, and they sensed that.

I sang in the church choir. My parents would take me to rehearsals and pick me up later. I remember that we got fifty cents each for singing in church on Sunday and another fifty cents every Wednesday night for coming to choir practice.

At rehearsal one night my friend Max Pool mentioned that he knew a boy who should be in our choir. "He's got a beautiful voice," Max said. "I'm going to bring him to practice some day." The following week, Max kept his word, and Bob Sanford came into my life.

Bob lived with his family on a farm between Independence and Coffeyville. He was two years older than me, and though I had passed him in the halls and we had been on school trips together, we had never really met.

I was attracted to him right away. He was about an inch taller than me—about five nine—had black hair, blue eyes, a ruddy complexion, and a beautiful speaking voice. He was slender but well-built, and I thought, handsome as any movie or TV star.

44

I was a high school sophomore then and as romantic as any dream-spinning girl my age. Bob's baritone blended perfectly with my mezzo-soprano, and I would imagine the two of us singing duets and smiling at each other tenderly as we sang, like Nelson Eddy and Jeanette MacDonald. Any romance was strictly in my mind, however, because Bob didn't ask for a date. At least, not until an eternity later. When you're sixteen and dying for a boy to ask you out, eternity is about three months.

I'll never forget how excited I was when he finally called. It was the summer before my junior year. He had just graduated.

The telephone rang on a hot August Sunday, and I picked it up. "Are you busy tonight, Charlotte?" It was Bob's voice.

I almost dropped the receiver. I'd planned some snappy replies in my daydreaming, but when the big moment arrived all I could do was mumble something about no special plans.

"Would you like to go to the drive-in," Bob asked. I think I said something great like, "Uh-huh," but Bob understood and was just as laconic.

"Eight o'clock," he said and hung up.

I spent the rest of the day racing around like mad to get ready. I couldn't get my hair just right so Mother gave me a quick permanent, and I set my hair a new way.

I pulled every dress I owned out of the closet and tried on each one. I wanted to look exactly right. Mother and I finally settled on a turquoise and white halter dress with a full skirt gathered at the waist.

Bob arrived promptly at eight. He wore blue jeans and a blue and white checked shirt. I could still see well enough to think he was Tony Curtis, Robert Walker, and a little of Gregory Peck.

Bob drove a 1936 Chevrolet. Now in those days, to have a car was something. Bob's family was really very poor,

45

but he needed a car because he lived in the country and had to go back and forth to town.

Jim Thorpe, All American was playing at the drive-in, and of course, I wouldn't see very much of what was happening on the screen from so far away.

I faked it. I kept my mouth shut except when I stuffed it full of popcorn, smiled, and pretended to follow the action closely. I'm pretty sure Bob knew I was putting on an act because much later he told me about a conversation he had had with his mother months before.

"My mother and I were driving behind your car after your first church solo," Bob recalled. "We could see you and your folks talking excitedly, about the performance I guess. Mother said how good you were. I remember my exact words then: 'The man who marries her will really have to be some man to accept that kind of responsibility.' "

So I know he was aware I really couldn't see the movie too well, but neither of us mentioned it. When it was time to go, Bob saw that one of the tires was flat, and he got down in the road to change it. Then he headed for a drive-in restaurant.

I remember the details of that evening even more clearly than my first date. I had a Seven-Up to drink, and we just sat and talked and talked and talked. Ask me about the conversation, and I'll repeat it back to you like a tape recorder. Through the open windows we could hear the strains of "Tenderly." Someone kept playing it over and over on the jukebox. For years afterward whenever I heard that tune I thought back to my first date with Bob. I think I probably fell in love with him that night. At least I began to, and it kept on growing. I'm not sure he felt that way right at the start because he took me home, thanked me, and didn't call again for about two months.

Bob belonged to 4-H, a club for kids interested in farming, and the following October he called to ask me to its Hallowe'en party in Independence.

46

Sallie Wyman, one of my close friends from school, was visiting, and she stared as I put down the phone and started racing around the room and squealing.

"What in the world is wrong with you, Charlotte?" she demanded. "You're acting very strange."

"He called again," I gasped. "He called again!"

"Who called?" she demanded. And I told her all about Bob. Then we both went straight for the closet to choose what I would wear. It wasn't to be a masquerade, just a dance or party, so we decided on a simple gray flared skirt and a frilly white blouse.

Hallowe'en night I came downstairs and pirouetted in front of Grandpa Akers who had come to live with us after Grandma had passed away.

"I know this boy, and he sure is nice," Grandpa Akers said. "But he's also mighty lucky to be taking out a girl as sweet and pretty as you."

Grandpa made me feel like a princess waiting to be swept up by her prince.

We dated on and off that year. Bob was going to Coffey-ville Community Junior College in town, and I was a junior in high school. He played basketball on the 4-H team, and I would go and sit in the grandstand and cheer madly when he scored, just like all the other girls who were watching their boyfriends.

I couldn't see the plays very well, but I learned to recognize him on the court by his shape and form. Other times I knew his voice and footsteps. He had a habit of clearing his throat in a certain way that I think was unconscious, but I always knew when he got out of the car and was coming to the door by that sound.

After the game, I would wait outside the lockers while Bob showered and changed, and then we would go out for a Coke. One cold February night, Bob took me home and kissed me goodnight. Then he reached for my hand and folded my fingers around his class ring.

47

"What does this mean?" I asked.

"What do you want it to mean?" he answered. He would never come right out and say anything. I assumed he wanted to go steady, but I wanted to hear the words.

I repeated, "I don't know what it means." Finally he said it: "Would you go steady with me?" I said yes before the words were out of his mouth. In my mind, I was already planning what I would wear to school the next day.

Those days a girl would wear her boyfriend's ring dangling from a velvet ribbon around her neck. I had a black and cream plaid skirt, a cream sweater, and a black velvet ribbon. I decided that outfit really showed off my ring, and I set off to school gaily.

The big social event of the high school year was the junior-senior prom, and I asked Bob to be my escort. Mother worked for weeks on my formal. It had a tight bodice and a full circle skirt covered with one-inch ruffles. It was beautiful, and I felt beautiful in it. I know Bob was proud of me. I kept him waiting with Dad quite a long time until I came down. When I apologized, Bob said gallantly, "It was worth waiting for."

That, from my silent swain! I knew he was really pleased. We were both in great spirits and, as they say in love stories, danced until dawn.

That summer Bob and I both got jobs at the Tackett Theater, one of Coffeyville's two movie houses. Bob worked as an usher. I sold tickets at the box office until about nine or nine-thirty, and then I had to balance out the money. The manager knew about my vision but gave me the job anyway. I never made a mistake, peering closely at the money handed me and the change I returned. At the close, I always balanced out to the penny.

Some nights I would stay to see the second movie and wait until Bob closed up. Then we might go out for a soda, or he would just take me home. Other nights Mother would walk down to meet me, and we'd go home together. Dad had a bread route then, and he had to be up at 3:30 A.M. to make his deliveries; but my folks didn't want me to walk home alone, so Mother came.

That was my first job. I only got paid seventy-five cents an hour, but it was a great learning experience. The lady I worked for was very exacting, and that's the best kind of boss to have. Looking back, I can see that the training that came from satisfying the demands of a tough employer helped build the self-discipline I needed later on.

I still had a year of high school to complete when Bob left Coffeyville to attend Kansas State University in Manhattan, and we continued our courtship through the mails. Bob would write real big, knowing how large to make the letters from the size of the ones in my letters to him.

After finishing high school, I enrolled in the junior college in town. Sight or no sight, I hoped to become a social worker. Bob, who was taking courses in agricultural economics, came down from Kansas State as often as he could, and we would go out and sit and talk for hours. Talk and smooch. He told me with quiet pride one evening that he had been elected to Farmhouse, an honorary fraternity at land-grant colleges. Extra smooching because of that, although by then we didn't need any reasons.

One day, on a visit back home, he held out his fraternity pin. Wordlessly. My heart did a flip-flop because every girl knew that being pinned was as close to an engagement as you could get. I was simply dying to grab it and put it on, but I told him he would have to get my father's permission. Bob swallowed hard and went to find Dad. Soon he came back and told me what Father told him.

"You can let her wear your pin, young feller," Father said, with mock seriousness, "and I know what in blazes that means. But if you get her pregnant I'll come after you with a shotgun!"

Before I was allowed to take courses in a social work major, I had to complete the basics, such as English composition, literature, math, speech, a few sciences. Readers helped me through. Sometimes friends would volunteer to read for me; other times my parents would pay readers seventy-five cents an hour.

Sometimes a reader would put a whole book on tape, and when it was time for me to read a special chapter, I would listen to just that section. I could replay it as often as I needed to. At other times, especially if the material was something I had to have for the next day's assignment, it would be read to me immediately. I would tape it and thus could relisten if necessary.

Research papers were done the same way. I would decide what books I needed, then the material was recorded. I played the tapes and "wrote" my paper—again on a tape. Later, I would have somebody type the manuscript so I could submit it to my professors. It took a lot more time to write a paper that way, but I was able to complete every one of my assignments.

Sometimes I tried to take notes in class and have them recorded, but my handwriting was pretty illegible; and this wasn't too satisfactory. My dad got me a small reel-to-reel recorder which I could carry to class. I got permission to record the lectures, and that worked best of all.

That first year, at Christmas of 1954, Bob and I officially became engaged. He came home for the holidays and almost immediately handed me a velvet box. It contained a small diamond solitaire, and I was so thrilled you'd have thought he had given me the Cullinan diamond. Much later, Bob told me ruefully, "It may not have been very big, but it took me a year to pay for it."

In September of 1955, I transferred to Kansas State University in Manhattan, about 200 miles to the northwest. The 153-acre campus on the northwest corner of the city, with its carefully planned landscaping, is stunningly beautiful. But to me it looked almost dreamlike on first view. The grass was blocks of green, the trees shadowy hulks rising from the green carpets and piercing the hard blue sky, the low ivied buildings, of limestone from the Fort Riley quarries, blurry patches of gray.

For the new girls, the first, and most important, event on campus was Rush Week—visiting the various sororities to decide which they want to join. And, at the same time, the sororities decide if they want the applicants. It's a scary procedure, and I'm not at all sure I approve of it now. A negative vote can leave a permanent scar on the vulnerable psyche of a young girl who had her heart set on a special house.

I decided to pledge Alpha Delta Pi and waited tensely for the answer. Would they want me? Especially, would they want a member with such limited vision? I wasn't certain if the girls knew about my sight and was equally uncertain about whether I should tell them. One night, before the acceptances were announced, one of the girls came over to me before a program started. "Charlotte," she asked me, "would you like to come up here and sit closer so you can see better?"

So they knew. But it didn't matter to them because I received a bid. Elated, I accepted and moved into the rambling old house on Sorority Row. Meanwhile, Bob, who was living in his frat house, would come over as often as he could to read for me. One of my sorority sisters helped too, and I engaged others as I needed them.

By this time, at the age of nineteen, I was considered to be legally blind. There was a state program, called Rehabilitation for the Blind, which would pay all college costs for blind students. I would have been eligible, but Dad wouldn't hear of it, believing anything like that smacked of welfare. A proud man, he did not want me to ask about it.

One day a representative of the agency came to our house. I don't know how he heard about me, but he talked to Mother and Daddy about this program and convinced them that it wasn't welfare at all, that our tax money had gone into this, and, most importantly, that it would be helping me.

I think that is what really did it. Daddy would do anything to help me. So they agreed that I could accept this money, and after that all the costs, readers and everything else, were paid for by the Rehabilitation for the Blind.

Now I really began to get into my courses. They were all about social problems, and that's what I wanted to do. I took psychology courses, basic psychology, abnormal psychology, sociology, carrying twelve hours a semester, not a full load but tough enough.

Bob finished school and went into the Army Reserve. He would be on active duty for six months and, after that, report for monthly drills and two weeks of summer camp for the next five years. He was stationed at Camp Chaffee, Arkansas, and Fort Leonard Wood, Missouri, quite a distance from home; and he didn't get back too often. I did visit him a couple of times. His parents had a friend who lived close to Fort Leonard Wood, and I stayed with her once. I also had a cousin nearby and would go there; Bob would come from camp, and so we could be together.

Meanwhile, I was back at Kansas State for my senior year. But this time I was alone. Bob was a long way off, and it was very different for me. I went through Rush Week—this time on the other side—and helped pledge the new sorority sisters. But I never really unpacked and moved in. I was homesick, and I missed Bob too much.

This was a low point in my life. I wandered around the campus desolately, unable to concentrate on my courses. Finally I called home, and I was crying.

"I just can't do it," I told my folks. "I can't stay here by myself." So I came home and lived with my folks again. I worked at the theater two or three nights a week and on weekends.

Bob and I had already set a wedding date, December 28, 1957, and I was glad to be able to spend this time with my parents and plan my wedding. With Bob away in the army, I had to do most of the planning by myself, but I didn't care. Hadn't I been dreaming about this for a long time? I knew exactly how I wanted everything to be done.

Chapter Five

I'm a winter person. I hate the hot weather. I didn't want to perspire, with my hair straggly as it often gets when the temperature is way up there. So it had to be a winter wedding because I wanted everything, especially me, to be perfect on my wedding day.

I chose December because of the love I have always felt in me and around me at that time of year. Everyone is more loving, more giving, and kinder in December; and I thought it would be a beautiful time to begin to share my life with Bob.

That date would also fit well into the pattern we were planning. Bob would be released from the army then, and it would be between semesters at school. We could get married, go on a honeymoon, and get settled in an apartment near the college in Manhattan so I could complete school.

That summer before we married, Mother and Dad sat up late one night, talking. Years later, Mother reconstructed the scene for me.

"The lights will go out soon, won't they?" Mother said. It was more a statement than a question.

Dad pressed his lips together and didn't answer for a while. Then he hit the arm of his chair, leaning forward, startling Mother. "Before they do," he said, leaning forward, "before her eyes go, let her see something she'll remember the rest of her life."

Mother smiled and, almost in unison, they said: "New York City!"

Mother's smile faded. "But it will be terribly expensive, and Howard, we don't have the money."

"Don't worry about the money," Dad replied. "My credit's damn good." He meant that for one of the few times in his life, he would borrow the money.

Next morning they told me. Talk about jumping for joy! I literally leaped in the air. So off we went, the three of us, to the great metropolis where an uncle, Dr. Milton Akers, was a well-known educator.

New York City! I could hardly believe it. I lived in a town of 12,000 and knew New York City only from the movies, but in my mind I had an exciting picture of sky-high buildings, streets crowded with busy, hurrying people, fast-moving cars. My uncle, who was the principal of a private, progressive school, the Walden School, lived in a penthouse atop a tall apartment house. I couldn't wait to get there.

Of course, my wedding was still very much in my thoughts. Wasn't New York City the hub of fashion, the place where all the glamorous models and luxurious fashions were? Although my mother was going to make my wedding dress, as she had made my dresses all of my life, I planned to scour the city for the most beautiful fabric I could find.

That New York trip was another example of the way my parents tried to make my life a pleasant happening. And it was! We went all over—Radio City, the Empire State Building, Grant's Tomb, up to the Cloisters, that exquisite building full of medieval art, Broadway. Uncle Milton had tickets for two Broadway shows. We saw Rosalind Russell in *Auntie Mame* and *Most Happy Fella*.

My uncle had some close friends in the building, a delightful Jewish couple who heard about my upcoming wedding and suggested I visit what they called "the garment district." They were sure I would find all kinds of wonderful materials there for my dress.

It was a fascinating place. Buildings full of dresses, coats, suits, every kind of clothing imaginable. Streets lined with stores selling not only fabric but buttons, trimmings, linings, thread, everything needed to make all these clothes. And worming their way through the crowds were young men pushing racks of clothing from factory to warehouse or truck.

In a tiny store, almost hidden from the street, in the basement of a dingy old church, I found what I was looking for. There were bolts of piece goods stacked from floor to ceiling—satins, silks, chiffons, velvets, every fabric imaginable and in a rainbow of colors. As soon as my fingers made contact with a length of velvet the storekeeper pulled from the pile, I knew this was to be it. We bought the most beautiful, softest white velvet for my wedding dress. The material for my attendants' dresses, a deep rose-red velvet, also came from the same magical pile.

One incident marred our New York trip. Dad used some of his borrowed money to buy me a pair of binoculars at Macy's. He wanted me to have the best possible sight of everything.

One morning, we visited my uncle's school on the west side of Manhattan, and those days we were able to park right in front. The binoculars and our camera were on the back seat, clearly visible, so we locked the doors before we went in. That's what we would have done back home.

We were in the school for about three hours. When we came out, the car had been broken into, and the camera and binoculars were gone. There were some teenage boys hanging around on the steps, and my uncle questioned them. But we were not able to get any clues so we just decided it was a lost cause. That part of living in a big city is certainly different from small-town life.

When we returned home, we were immediately caught up in plans for the wedding. Mother started work on my dress right away, and I hung over her shoulder, watching. It had a princess skirt and a low, sweetheart neckline, with pleats in the back that extended into a long train. My attendants wore identical dresses without the train.

That dress. What a story that is. Mother finished it about three months ahead of time. It was perfect. I remember how proud she was and how excited we all were. Of course, we didn't let Bob see it—that would have been bad luck. Mother hung it in a plastic bag, and Dad carried it to the attic.

About two weeks before the wedding, I was scheduled to have my portrait taken. Dad got the dress from its storage place and took it to the cleaner's to be steamed and pressed because it had become wrinkled after having hung in the closet so many months.

On the day of the picture-taking, Dad dropped Mother and me at the studio and went for the dress. We were still at the photographer's when he returned, and I'll never forget his face. He looked stricken. Wordlessly, he held up the dress, and then it was our turn to look stricken. And horrified.

At the cleaner's, they had put the dress on a form to steam it smooth but had left it on too long. The dress was a total disaster. It had shrunk at least three sizes and was a mass of wrinkles, perfect for cutting up and using as a dust cloth. It certainly would never be a wedding dress again. One glance told Mother and me that the dress was too far gone for restoration.

There were so many details left to deal with and, on top of everything else, no wedding dress with the ceremony only two weeks off. It was a crisis of major proportions.

But we Kansans are equal to anything. Well, maybe some other Kansans, because I admit I was in shock for a while. Next day, some friends, less emotionally involved than I, took charge. "Come on," they told Mother and me. "We're going to Tulsa." Mother and I got into the car and drove the eighty miles to the city where, in no time at all, we bought another piece of white velvet. It wasn't as soft and silky as the original piece, but it would have to do.

Back home, Mother girded for the race against the calendar. Dad was Gloomy Gus, pessimistic about her chances of finishing it in time; but Mother just stitched away, hour after hour, determined to duplicate the ruined dress.

And she did. The morning of the wedding, she put the final stitch in the hem, and I had my beautiful dress again. Dad switched, as men will, and took some of the credit. "I knew you'd do it," he told Mother proudly.

We had the rehearsal for the ceremony on a Friday evening, the night before my wedding day. I was pretty much in charge because, with Bob away all those months, I had gone over all the details in my mind many times. I knew how I wanted everybody in the wedding party to come in, where they were to stand and where to sit. I made them all go through their paces three or four times until I was satisfied.

After the rehearsal, we went back to my home for drinks and snacks. It was customary in our town for the parents of the groom to give a rehearsal dinner; but Bob's family was not well off financially, and his mother had been quite ill, so my folks invited everybody back informally. We had a fine time. Everybody felt great that all the preparations had been made and we could finally relax.

The evening of our wedding day was cold and clear. Our church holds around four or five hundred persons, and there wasn't an empty seat. The lady who made the floral centerpieces and the bouquets was helping to arrange my train when she said to me, "Charlotte, I've never seen a more beautiful bride."

Well, I'm sure there were more physically beautiful brides, but inside, at that moment, I was the fairest of them all because I know all the beauty and love I felt must have been shining through.

Over my dress floated a veil of bridal illusion attached to a tiara headpiece studded with pearls and sequins. I wore satin slippers with low heels because Bob and I were the same height and I didn't want to tower over my bridegroom. I carried a bouquet of white gardenias and red roses, and my three attendants carried nosegays of the white and red flowers pinned to white fur muffs. They were my best friends in high school—Sallie Wyman, my maid of honor, and Sarah Jo Persley and Ruth Bowen, who were the bridesmaids. Joyce, who was very pregnant, presided over the guest book. Two days later, she had her baby.

While the guests were assembling in the church, the strains of an organ filled the air. I had selected the music carefully—"Our Love," based on a theme from Tchaikovsky's *Romeo and Juliet,* and "How Do I Love Thee," from the poem by Elizabeth Barrett Browning.

Dad and I paused at the head of the aisle. It was dark outside, but the church was ablaze with light. Dozens of candles flanked both sides of the altar, and there were huge, lighted tapers along the aisle on each pew.

I glanced sideways at my dad and wondered what he was thinking. I knew fathers always hate to give up their little girls. But did my dad have a special sadness? He knew someday I would be blind. Did he wonder whether Bob would love and cherish me as he and Mother had always loved and cherished each other?

As for me, I had no doubts or reservations. A number of my married women friends have asked me: "Didn't you have second thoughts? At the last minute, when you were walking down the aisle or saying your vows, weren't you scared?"

These girls, who didn't face the the possibility of a handicap as I did, admitted to having last-minute worries, but I can honestly say I had none. The need I felt to give my life to Bob was genuine and complete. Even the knowledge that someday I would not be able to see did not frighten me.

Bob and I had discussed this often before our marriage.

I knew that Bob's father had talked to him and had said, "Are you sure you want to do this? It is hard enough to make a marriage work, but it's even harder when one of the people is handicapped.

"You know what's going to happen. Do you really know what you're doing?" he asked. "Do you really know?"

Bob said, "Yes."

Once we were sitting in his car and began to talk frankly about the possibility of my blindness. It was night-time, and we were looking at the stars. Bob said I would always see the world and its beauty through his eyes. "I'll describe things to you," he explained. "I'll show them to you as I see them, and they will be vivid and alive."

Bob's words were in my ears as Dad and I walked slowly down that aisle to meet him. I knew that the faith I had which had been with me every step of the way would always be there. I felt that as long as you cling to your belief in Jesus Christ and as long as you have people around you, loving you, you can face anything.

The ceremony took only about fifteen minutes. It was very traditional. Back in those days, you didn't do your own thing and add anything to the old words. The organ played softly throughout the service, "Clair de Lune" by Debussy, and Bob and I exchanged rings. Mine matched the engagement ring he had given me.

There's a funny story about the ring I chose for Bob. Before I went to the jeweler's, I asked him if he had any special preferences. Bob said he had admired a faceted band worn by one of his friends. He described it as looking like a nut on a bolt, and drew a picture for me.

I nodded and went into the store but with little real notion of what I was looking for. "I want a man's wedding ring," I told the smiling salesman. "But it has to be a band that looks like a bolt." His smile faded, and he appeared startled. "A bolt?" he asked incredulously. "You mean something . . . something sticking up?" He paused, thoroughly flustered. Had I realized what I was saying, I would have blushed crimson.

"A bolt," I repeated firmly, and drew from memory the picture Bob had scratched on a pad for me. I heard the salesman sigh visibly as he said: "Oh, you mean a nut." He brought out a few, and I made my selection.

Being short of both time and money, we hadn't planned an elaborate wedding trip. "After all," I teased Bob, "won't our whole life be a honeymoon?" But we did plan to go to Kansas City for three or four days. Sallie was student teaching there, and her apartment was vacant during the Christmas vacation. She offered it to us, and we accepted.

I had chosen my going-away outfit carefully. I wore a black wool suit, trimmed with brown mink. All the accessories, hat, shoes, pocketbook, and gloves, were black. Mother, of course, had objected to the color. "Nobody chooses black for a going-away outfit," she said. But I did. And I thought I looked stunning. So did Bob.

We started out with a full gas tank and thirty-five dollars—ten of which had been given to Bob by my father as we left the church. Years later, Bob said, "I sure was glad to see that ten-dollar bill. I knew we had a place to stay and gas in the car; but we had to eat for three days, and I wondered if we would be able to make it."

Sallie and Norman Benzinger, the best man, led us to where he had hidden our car, a 1951 gun-metal gray Ford. He had taken the precaution of hiding it to prevent anybody from decorating it with signs and cans. We drove off.

After driving a long distance, we realized neither of us had had anything to eat for hours. We tried to find a restaurant or coffee shop open; but it was late, and everything was shut up tight. Finally, we stopped at a little motel in Humboldt, Kansas, where we were able to get a room for the night. We split a Coke. There was nothing else around.

I went into the bathroom to prepare for bed, full of excitement and love for Bob. I arranged my hair and slipped into a nightgown of white chiffon and lace, carefully, so that I would not mess up the curls. I threw a matching robe around my shoulders and went into the bedroom where Bob waited for me.

Soon we became one in the beautiful way that love is shared in a marriage.

We woke up about eleven o'clock the next morning, ravenous. Outside, as we went to our car, we burst into laughter. There were seven cars lined up in the parking lot. Each had a "Just Married" sign attached to the bumper. Evidently we had all been married the night before and found our way to this tiny little motel in the town of Humboldt.

It was Sunday, and we had to drive a few miles to the next town before we could get some food. By this time, we had missed breakfast completely, so we went into a hotel restaurant and had a turkey dinner. We pretended we were having our first Christmas dinner together.

Sallie's place in Kansas City was tiny and a delightful place for two people to begin their life together. There were two small rooms, a compact kitchen, and a living room with a Murphy bed which was pulled down from the wall at night.

We were so happy and so close and so much in love in that tiny borrowed apartment. It was bitterly cold in Kansas City, with a strong penetrating wind, but we didn't let that bother us. We walked the street hand in hand, sat close together in the movies, made love a lot. Once we went to a nightclub, a fancy dinner and dancing place. There was a maid in the ladies' room to hand out towels and help you with your hair. She said to me, "Honey, you look beautiful!" I guess she could see that I was in love and felt loved in return.

Bob and I began our married life in a basement apartment in a ramshackle building in Manhattan, Kansas, where

I was to continue my schooling and he had a job selling shoes. It was pretty awful—concrete floors, green walls with flaking plaster, and wooden frame furniture with upholstered pillows. In the winter months plastic was taped to the windows to keep out the drafts.

Mother made curtains, but there wasn't too much we could do to beautify it. Bob would describe our color scheme as a "brilliant shade of vomit." Of course, we paid only forty-two dollars a month for rent, including utilities, so maybe we shouldn't have expected too much.

I can remember when we had lived in Manhattan before we were married, when we were dating, and he was in his fraternity house and I was in my sorority house, how I used to dream of the time when we would be together. Well, I told Bob, "Maybe it is just two rooms, and maybe they are not the most beautiful two rooms in the world; but I'm happy."

That spring of 1958 I wasn't feeling well, and finally one of my readers at the University took me to a doctor. After an examination, the doctor said I wasn't sick, probably just a little pregnant. Three or four days later a test confirmed his diagnosis. I didn't tell Bob immediately, although I was almost bursting with joy at this secret. I waited for the "right moment." In the movies, it was always done at a candlelight dinner or some other romantic setting, and I was looking for one.

Well, mine came in the middle of the afternoon while we were sitting outside an apartment building in Bob's car trying to decide on an apartment.

We had been hunting for a place to live for weeks. While Bob had been at his army camp for two weeks, I had gone home. On our return, we found that things in our basement apartment had mildewed. There was a dampness and an odor I could not tolerate, especially when I began to have morning sickness.

We looked at many apartments, and some of them

were pretty depressing. Finally, sitting in the car that day I said, "Honey, I sure hope this is going to be the right place because there's going to be more than just the two of us now. We're going to have a baby."

I can remember vividly how he just took me in his arms and kissed me. It was a beautiful moment. We didn't have the soft music or the candlelight, but we had each other and the blessing of a first child on the way. On that lovely spring day, that was our "right moment."

We never did complete that apartment hunt. With my severely limited vision, we decided that motherhood and a student's life didn't go together. We decided to return home to Coffeyville.

Bob wisely went ahead before we moved to job-hunt. In no time, he landed one in a department store, a shoe salesman at sixty-five dollars a week. He came back all smiles. It was, for those days and for us, a tremendous salary.

We rented a U-Haul trailer, loaded all our possessions on it, and came home. We would stay with my parents until we could find a place of our own.

Of course, I adored being back with my parents. We had always been very close, and I had been homesick while I was at Kansas State. So Bob and I got settled in, he at his new job and I busy with preparations for our baby. Mother and I would go shopping for diapers and shirts and sweaters and everything we could think of. We knew I would have a winter baby, and we bought enough warm things for a whole nursery.

The months flew by. We decided to name the baby after my cousin, Steven Rauch, fourteen years younger than I, who was almost like my own little brother from the time he was born. Of course, Steve became Stephanie when our expected son turned out to be a daughter. I remembered the little girl Stephanie who had stood on her head in Sunday School years before and smiled to myself.

Stephanie was scheduled to arrive on Christmas Eve

but didn't make it. She was born two weeks late. That was probably the worst part of my whole pregnancy. The labor pains just didn't start so the doctor ordered castor oil and quinine for me. Still nothing happened, so I had to take that awful mess again. I don't think either of the doses had any effect, other than to make me sicker than I already was.

I think when it was time for her to come, she just came on her own. We finally went to the hospital on January 8, around 10:30 P.M., a terribly cold, snowy night. Bob drove very slowly and carefully while I sat in the back seat with Mother.

I went directly to the maternity floor, and when I stepped off the elevator, one of the nurses on duty said, "Well, we've been looking for you. It's about time you got here."

That's the beautiful part about living in a small town. People know and care about you. I've always felt loved in this community. I know people were interested in my problems and wanted to help. For the past few months, I had been taking the hospital's courses on prenatal and infant care, and so the personnel knew me and were watching for me when the baby was due.

She wasn't born for about twenty-four hours, and meantime my entire family had gathered in the hospital's waiting room. And when my family gathers, it's quite a crowd. "You wouldn't believe that room downstairs," one of the nurses said.

I knew all this and it helped allay the last-minute fear which I think I had in common with all young girls.

"What would the pain of childbirth be like?" I wondered. "Will I be able to handle it?" Again, my answer came from my love for Bob and my faith in God. As long as we were doing this together and I was having his child, I would be able to handle it. And with God's help, I did.

All of my life, whenever I had been ill, my eyes were affected and my sight worsened. The moments right after childbirth, I could hardly see at all. Everything was in shadow.

The nurse came into my room carrying a white bundle. She held it up and said, "Charlotte, this is your little girl." All I could really see was a red blob at the top of the bundle, and that was her face.

I was heavily sedated so the nurse did not let me hold the baby. I remember that fleeting look was followed almost immediately by a sensation of love I think only a mother could understand. It was a beautiful, fulfilling love, and I thanked God for helping Bob and me to produce another of His miracles.

I stayed in the hospital longer than most women because it was a little harder for me to learn to handle the baby, and I didn't seem to recuperate as fast. The beds were very narrow, and I didn't move a muscle when I held Stephanie. I didn't want to drop her. The nurses were very careful too. They always put up the sides of my bed when I had the baby, and there was always someone in the room with us.

Years later I became friendly with a woman who had been in the maternity ward when I was. She came to me one day, and she confessed, "I didn't know you then and I didn't know you were blind. I almost hated you because all the nurses seemed to hover over you and your baby, and none of us knew why.

"We were put out. Because we were there with our new babies also, and our babies were special too. I want to apologize now because I didn't know you couldn't see."

Obviously a lot of the other mothers didn't know either. I didn't want to seem different; but I did require extra help, and I was sorry if it took the nurses away from the others. Actually, when I held the baby, I was never really conscious there was anybody else in the room. My entire being was focused on the baby in my arms.

When it was time to go home, both Bob and Dad came

for us. Dad kept the car warm so that the baby would not get chilled, and Bob came up to the maternity floor. We left the hospital with Stephanie cradled in Bob's right arm and me clinging to his left.

I glowed. I was a mother now.

Chapter Six

Spring arrived but with raw, blustery winds. Each morning, on awakening, I peered outside, hoping a warm day had dawned, warm enough to put Stephanie in a carriage and wheel her around the block, like all the other proud mothers.

I could still walk alone, unaided. I was doing all my daily chores around the house. No problem there, though they got done a bit more slowly. Bob and I lived and loved like many other young married couples in town.

March finally ended its dreary days, and soon, I thought, the warm days would come. But April was wet and dismal. Still, I kept hoping.

When April was a week old, I awoke one morning to the sound of raindrops again. I turned to the window, but it wasn't there. Frightened, I turned toward the crib. There was no crib, only darkness. A little frantic, I turned my head and looked around the room, searching for familiar objects. I looked but saw nothing. I could not even make out the once-blurry outlines of the bed from which I had just risen, the dresser, the chairs.

Suddenly, a chill went through me.

During the night, I had lost what little vision had remained. All that was left was the barest perception of light in my left eye. The right eye had been totally blind since I was sixteen. I groped toward the window, leaned on the sill, and stared. There was a vague lightness, but nothing else.

Finally it had come. I was blind. At twenty-three, with a three-month-old baby.

With the full realization of what happened came the fears. "Dear God," I whispered. "How am I ever going to satisfy my husband? And how am I ever going to take care of my baby?"

I got out of bed and went upstairs to the bathroom—there was only one in the house—to wash and dress. I put on slacks and a shirt, combed my hair, and brushed my teeth. By this time the baby had awakened, and Mother had given her a bottle. I walked into the kitchen and took my place at the breakfast table. I guess I had operated more by feel than I realized because I knew exactly where to go. I felt for my fork. Yes, there it was. Nobody sensed that anything was changed.

I knew I couldn't hide it. But I just couldn't bring myself to say the words.

But it had to be done. Finally, after five agonizing minutes had passed, I simply said, "When I woke up this morning I could not see." Bob's hand quickly reached out to cover mine. I could hear raindrops hit the window but no other sound. No one said anything. No one knew what to say or do. I can't remember whether I cried, but I'm sure there were tears in my parents' eyes. We had all known it might happen; we were all prepared. But when it became a reality, we could hardly believe it.

Bob said: "I'll call the store and tell them I won't be in today."

"No!" I said, perhaps louder than I had intended. "No," I said again, more quietly. He must go to work, I told him. Just like on any other day. Things mustn't change.

At first Bob wouldn't hear of leaving me that first day, but I was adamant. Something told me we had to keep our lives on an even keel right from the start. When he saw that I meant it, Bob reluctantly kissed me good-by and left. I heard his footsteps all the way down the path. Later, he was to tell me: "I was prepared, at least I thought I was. Bu when I heard you say, 'I can't see,' I felt as though I'd been hit by a hammer."

Upstairs Stephanie began squalling. Mother said she would take care of her.

I groped to the couch in the living room and sat down, my hands folded in my lap primly. My mind whirled. I knew I should do something, keep going; but I didn't know what, or how, at least just yet. I heard Dad's footsteps.

Poor Dad, he was so gentle and so worried. He reminded me of the evangelist who was speaking at the Episcopal Church. Dad took my hand.

"Charlotte, why don't you go talk to her and let her pray for you?" he asked.

His suggestion surprised me. Dad wasn't an outwardly religious man. He did go with me regularly to Sunday School and church, but he never quoted the Bible or said, "Let's go for prayer." But prayer had always sustained me in the past, so Dad, Grandpa, who had heard the news over the telephone and hurried over, and I got into the car to visit the evangelical minister.

Riding in the car, I looked out the window and strained to see something, anything. I blinked my eyes hard many times, and peered out the window. A sharp pain shot through my head, but I blinked hard again and again, trying desperately to restore the little vision I had left. But I saw nothing.

When we got to the church, Dad took my arm to help me out of the car and up the steps. We were both awkward and clumsy. Dad and the other members of my family soon learned how to help me without calling attention to my blindness.

The evangelist, whose name was Agnes Sanford (no relation to Bob's family), was waiting for us in a small pine-paneled office in the church.

I stood awkwardly, holding Dad's arm. "Sit down, dear," she said to me. I heard a chair being moved. I put my hand behind me, feeling the arms, feeling the seat, and slowly lowered myself into it. I heard the scraping of another chair and felt Dad's hand on mine. He was seated beside me.

In a low voice, the evangelist asked me about my eyes. I told her all I could remember about my life, my eye condition, the doctors, everything. Dad filled in what I did not remember.

She listened carefully, saying little. When we had finished, she said: "Your father and I will read from the Scripture." She turned to one of my favorite passages from St. John, 14:1. I knew it by heart and recited along with them: "Let not your heart be troubled; ye believe in God, believe also in me."

Then she asked if we would like to pray.

Many people are skeptical about prayers, about whether they are heard, whether they are answered, whether they are, in fact, needed at all.

I believe, fully and completely, in the power of prayer.

Prayer is not merely asking God for *things*—for anything from a way out of trouble to material objects. It is a way of communicating with God personally, of being with and coming closer to Him.

And prayer is not just the words that are spoken. It is the feeling inside that accompanies them. Merely saying words ritualistically, without thinking about them, understanding them, and meaning them is not praying at all. It is paying lip service to religion.

I did not pray for instant healing. God does not grant us our prayers before we are ready for them. The answers must be left to God. Frequently, there will indeed be an answer to our prayers, though not in the specific way we expect or want. For example, God may give to us some wonderful opportunities to do things which would be even better than the things we are asking for.

The overridingly important point to bear in mind as we pray are the four crucial words from the Lord's Prayer: "Thy will be done." That is the "bottom line." It means

71

simply that we should want what He wants rather than asking God to perform for us what *we* want.

I prayed for guidance and strength. And my prayers were indeed answered, almost at once. I felt God's arms around me. I felt His love and His toughness. I felt a peace and a joy suffuse my entire being.

I walked out of that office in the church more confident than I had walked in. I had always known that I, as a human being, could accomplish nothing alone but that with Jesus as my guide, my comforter, and my strength, I can endure. But now I felt it more keenly, *knew* it in the deepest part of me.

I knew also that I needed a lot of what is called "inner healing" to take place—the curing of the soul—before God could cure my body. I felt—I *knew*—the outer curing would take place, all in God's own good time.

The strength kept intensifying through that long, lonely day, ebbing a little at times but coming back more forcefully. When we returned home, I sat once more on the couch, folding clothes while Mother took care of Stephanie. Moments of doubt assailed me as I sat there, shaky moments when I wondered: "What am I going to do? How am I going to do it?"

But the strength of Jesus surged through.

By day's end, I knew I could no longer just sit there and fold clothes. I knew there was a purpose in life. I had a purpose to serve God; to serve Jesus Christ; to be a wife; to be a mother. No matter how hard it was, I knew I had to do it. Yes, my prayers had been answered, in God's own way.

I looked at the past, and I saw that things had been done to help me along the way. I knew that God would be there in the future. It wasn't going to be easy. It was going to be a whole new world, a harder world. It would take me longer to do things. There would have to be a big adjustment on my part, on my husband's part; but I knew within me—I had the calm assurance from God—that it would be all right, and I could make it with His help.

I think it was probably that day that I realized that my whole life would be a prayer. That day I knew utter dependence on a Being greater than I was. I realized that without Him I could do nothing. From that day on, my life has been a communication with Jesus Christ. On that lonely day when the dark descended, I saw that He could sustain me in any situation.

I made a lot of decisions before the day ended. I didn't want to sit and receive pity. I wanted to do more with my life than that. I wasn't the kind of woman to feel sorry for myself because other mothers could see and I could not. I knew that I would be helped to do more through my love of God and my husband, my family, and a tiny little bundle in a cradle.

Chapter Seven

Something strange and quite wonderful happened when the light went out on the world outside. The illumination *within* me increased a dozen-fold. As my senses of touch, taste, smell, and hearing, acute from an early age, suddenly seemed to become more sensitive, my emotions deepened too.

Love for my home, my husband, my mother and father became more alive, more truly *real,* than ever before. It was God's way of setting me on a path to true beauty, to a true meaning of life itself, a meaning I probably would not have known had I not gone blind.

It did not happen at once, of course. But gradually, I came to realize that without the use of eyes, an individual can do a lot of existing. But without God, there is no existence.

Existence—living, loving, being an integral part of the world around us—does not stop when your eyes go, or your hearing goes, or you become paralyzed in any way, or when you can no longer move freely in the world. Not then do you stop existing. Only when Jesus Christ goes out of your life does existence grind to a halt.

At the same time, I was human, too, and proud.

I was blind yet I didn't want to *look* or *act* blind. As a child I had seen that sightless people tended to drop their heads when they walked and that they groped their way with a cane. I mean no disrespect for the sightless, God knows, but I wanted to appear normal to the rest of the world.

Most of all, I wanted to be perfectly capable of caring for my home and little family. I had a horror of becoming a burden to anybody. I was one of God's human beings, and I wanted to enjoy the life He had given me. I had feelings, wants, desires, physical desires that as a young woman were strong within me, and I wanted those desires, wants, and feelings fulfilled.

I would not be human if I did not feel resentful at times, resentful and bitter. There were indeed times when anger and rebellion welled up inside me, and I cried inwardly: "Why me? Why must I go through life raising a baby I could not see, loving a husband whose face I could not look upon, missing the sunrises and sunsets and all the breathtaking beauties of nature?"

There were times of self-pity, times of depression, times when the future stretching ahead seemed bleak and cheerless, an endless night, times when the dark descended not only outside me but began seeping into my mind as well.

And there were times when I had to call upon every ounce of inner strength I possessed to keep from going over the brink into an emotional darkness.

But that's getting ahead of my story.

There is much misunderstanding on the part of seeing people about what blindness really means and precisely what the world looks like to one who cannot see.

There are many definitions of blindness. Legally, a person is considered blind in the United States if he or she can see no more at a distance of twenty feet than someone with normal vision can see at 200 feet.

Medically, blindness is defined as irreversible and complete loss of sight. About 1,700,000 persons in this country are either legally blind or severely handicapped visually. Of this number, only about 400,000 have no usable sight at all.

I was classed as one of these because, while one eye was totally blind, I could make out some light—scarcely any but a little—with the other. But nothing else. The field of view for blind persons varies considerably. For me, it was not the blackness of being shut away in a closet but as though I were surrounded by a perpetual, dense, impenetrable fog. The tiny amount of light perception I had never increased as the years went on. Looking out an open door or window, I could not tell if the bare brightness I saw was the sun, the moon, or the headlights of an automobile.

I confess that it is only on recollection that I can even describe what it was like. For truthfully, I was not conscious of how things "looked." I was much too occupied with thinking and planning my every move.

The day after my sight went, Bob bought me a long white cane to sweep ahead of me when I walked. I used it for a few months but then took it out less and less frequently, finally discarding it altogether. I preferred to rely upon my four remaining senses.

After the first few days of blindness, I never groped but walked upright, shoulders back. I had two secrets which allowed me to do it. One was memory, which I will talk about in detail later. The other was Bob who, true to his promise, was my eyes.

We learned to do things together as though we were a trained vaudeville team. In no time, we had developed a set of signals. We would always walk together, my hand slipped lightly through his arm. We quickly learned to time our steps so that I would instantly know about obstacles. Instead of telling me, "Now, Charlotte, here's a curb coming up" or "there's a tree in your path," he would pause or gently veer away. I would know by the movement of his body next to mine exactly what he meant, and I would respond.

The hardest thing for me that first year was eating in public. I was terrified that I would make some dreadful mistake and create a mess that would embarrass Bob and my friends, not to mention me. The first few months I'd absolutely refuse to dine out. But after Bob and I had perfected our signals in that vital area too, I decided to take the plunge.

Our first experience was a roaring success. We were invited to dinner at a friend's home, and I dressed carefully, having learned to comb my hair and even apply little dabs of make-up. If I overdid the rouge, Bob would simply flip a tissue from a box and wipe off the excess without saying a word.

At dinner, we put our system into operation, and it worked fine. It was based on the hands of a clock. Bob would whisper to me: "Water glass at one o'clock, butter's at eleven." If I wanted a sip of water I'd reach out, even while turning my head the other way to catch what our host was saying, clasp the glass, and bring it to my lips. No problem. When the food arrived, Bob would inform me: "Green beans are at noon, small roast potatoes at six, and roast beef at three." I'd pick up my knife and fork and begin.

Nevertheless, I kept worrying about accidents. Wouldn't I make a fool of myself if I did something dreadful; would I hear ill-concealed snickers?

Well, it had to happen, and when it did it was a lulu.

Bob and I were at a dinner party where the talk turned to local elections which were dividing the community. I became intensely interested and broke into the conversation. "But there isn't a single thing in that man's entire record," I expostulated, "that even hints he can help our area. I can't for the life of me understand . . ."

I had, of course, been briefed by Bob, but I had become so worked up, our clock signals became scrambled in my mind. I stuck my fork into my roll and brought it to my mouth, banging my teeth, while with my right hand I picked up a fistful of mashed potatoes, sopping with gravy no less.

I could feel the blush of embarrassment creep up to my temples; I wanted to crawl into a deep hole somewhere. But nobody gave the slightest sign of noticing. I simply wiped my hand on my napkin, Bob slipped me a clean one, and the talk went on as though nothing had happened.

That broke the ice. Realizing that the sky wouldn't fall in, I no longer feared the possibility of social accidents. There were, I can assure you, plenty of others. Like biting into a butter knife thinking it was a carrot stick. Or sticking my finger into scalding hot tea or knocking over sugar bowls now and then. Nobody cared, and Bob, instead of studiously ignoring them, which would have made me feel bad, kidded me gently when they happened. "I hope you didn't put teeth marks into her good silver," he whispered to me after the butter knife episode. He got a sharp pinch on his knee for that, and we both giggled.

Once, during a refreshment break at a Bible study group, dessert was served on a doily made of silver foil. The dessert was delicious, but I couldn't say the same for the doily, part of which I ate before I realized what was happening. Neither was it much fun going through the remainder of the program surreptitiously trying to dislodge a piece of the silver that had lodged between my teeth and was hurting like the dickens.

Bob and I had a beautiful sexual relationship. There is a wonderful harmony in nature, in life itself; the harmony of physical union is no less perfect, when love is the accompaniment. Bob was an excellent lover, and with my sharpened senses, I responded completely and sublimely.

Before marriage, I had been, as all young girls are, curious about sex, the intensity of my interest heightening as my body developed and the hormones began pouring through it. But I had never dreamed that a sexual relationship could be so utterly perfect, so completely fulfilling.

We made love spontaneously. Our love-making was natural, it was joyous, it was thrilling, and it was frequent!

My earlier fears that I would go into hiding when the curtain came down on my sight were soon dispelled. Busy as I was with Steph and finding my way as a new mother, I found time to join a prayer group, to continue singing in the church choir, and to lead an active social life.

With my good friend Marilyn Lively, Joyce, and an older woman, we devised the idea of holding our prayer meetings just before dawn. That way, our husbands would still be home and our children in bed—so nobody would need sitters—and we wouldn't be missed. Every Tuesday, shortly before 5:00 A.M., I would slip out of bed, dress hurriedly, and, after a quick breakfast, would meet Joyce (who was now Joyce Logan) and walk out in the still air of early morning. It is a perfect time of day to meet with your Lord and have communion with Him. The world has not yet begun to stir, the cares of the day not yet started to press in upon us. Life lies quiescent, yet God's handiwork is around us, gentle as the call of the white-throated sparrow, as the dew on the grass beneath our feet, as the sweet scent of the leaves in the trees I passed. These are God's reminders that He is there, all about us. We would return home just before alarm clocks would rouse our families.

I also continued to play bridge, learn about infant and child care, give Bible lessons, and sing in the church choir.

Bob and I played with a group of friends twice a month after covered-dish dinners at each other's homes. After I had gone blind, they all thought I would have to drop out. Well, hardly.

I got a visit one day from a representative of an organization called Career Rehabilitation for the Blind, who asked me if I wanted to learn the Braille system of reading and writing. The technique, invented in the mid-nineteenth century by a Frenchman named Louis Braille who lost his sight after an accident, uses raised dots which form symbols on a special type of paper. The home teacher explained: "You can write Braille by using a stylus, something like a pencil, and a guide ruler with which to punch little pits into the paper. You read by moving your fingers along the lines. The entire English alphabet of 26 letters is formed by using different arrangements of just six dots.

"For example, a single dot is an 'a,' two vertical dots are a 'b,' two diagonal ones going from left to right are 'e' while two diagonal ones from right to left are 'i.' And so on. It's a lot like shorthand." The teacher explained that there is also a Braille method for writing and reading music, which he warned was highly complex, a Braille math code, and even a typewriter that writes in Braille.

I was surprised to learn that only about five percent of persons considered legally blind in the United States use Braille all or some of the time. The system, of course, is of great value to blinded people.

I was enthusiastic. "Let's get started," I said. But I must admit I got only as far as learning the difference between the jack of spades and the ten of clubs in a deck of cards. I mean that I learned just enough to "read" Braille cards so that I could continue playing bridge.

Later, I joined a mothers' study club where we exchanged ideas on child-rearing and heard speakers explain to us what to expect as our youngsters moved into each new phase of their lives.

Learning two or three new songs every week for the church choir was a tough nut to crack. But it was learn or leave, and I loved singing too much to quit, so I looked for—and soon found—a solution. I listened for a woman in the choir who had an exceptionally strong voice, and edged my way next to her. As she sang, I would listen closely, and after three or four go-rounds I'd have the song memorized.

So I got through the first six months of my blindness with few major crises.

Then, abruptly, I came face to face with one.

When Stephanie was nine months old, I learned that another baby was on the way. Taking care of one was difficult enough. Would I be able to handle *two?*

Lying in bed, I did some mental arithmetic. My second baby would arrive when Steph was only eighteen months old, still in the wobbly yet adventurous stage when bumps and tumbles would be frequent, nearing the time when she would be darting all over the place, exploring her glorious new world with vast curiosity.

Questions tumbled through my mind. Would I be able to anticipate and guard against the dangers into which her immaturity could lead her? Would I be able to protect her while at the same time giving her the freedom without which she might erupt into rebellious behavior? Would I be able to teach, feed, bathe this squirmy, active little person who, I remembered from our mothers' study group, was also entering upon the negativistic or "no" stage?

The responsibility would be almost overwhelming, and while I would be attempting to cope with it, a new baby, needing all the loving care it could get, would arrive in the household.

We were living with my parents and of course that helped. But to make ends meet, my mother had to work. I would be alone with my babies all day long.

I lay in bed, eyes wide open, staring into the darkness. Tears ran down the sides of my face and dampened the pillow. "God," I whispered, "how am I ever going to do it? *How am I going to do it?* Please be with me."

Beside me, Bob stirred in his sleep. I continued to pray silently until I guessed morning was near, when I fell into a fitful sleep. Soon the alarm rang, and the day had begun.

The thoughts were with me all that day. Late in the afternoon, Dad came home from work and saw me sitting glumly in the rocking chair, feeding Steph.

I heard his steps come to a halt near me. A pause. I knew he was looking down at me. Then his voice, sounding worried, came to my ears. "Charlotte. What's happened?" I looked up at the voice.

"Daddy," I said, my voice quavering. "How am I going to do it? Two babies, Daddy. Two babies!"

There was silence. Then the voice came again, and this time the concern had changed to a suspicion of sternness.

"Charlotte," it said.

"Yes, Daddy," I replied, looking up.

"You have two arms, don't you?" A shuffle as he turned. Gradually diminishing sounds of footsteps as he left the room.

I knew what he meant. I had two arms and I could hold two babies. It was much later that I learned Dad was even more apprehensive about the coming problem than I, but he knew that he could not, should not, transmit that worry to me. He must at all costs show his full faith and confidence in my ability to fulfill my responsibilities. Mother, too, exuded a sunny confidence that she wasn't really feeling and so did Bob. Had any one of them showed doubt, my rapidly shredding self-confidence would have become unraveled completely.

Confidence, like happiness, is contagious. I could easily have tormented myself by self-doubt into a state of actual helplessness in which I could be almost literally paralyzed by my fears. But the confidence of my family was a stone wall that kept that sickly self-pity from rushing at me in a torrent and engulfing me.

All of a sudden, I knew I could do it. I knew I had a strong young husband. I knew I did have two good arms! And I knew that God would be there. My confidence zoomed like a rocket off to the moon. I began to look forward to the arrival of my new baby.

To make room for her (or him) my parents decided to buy a new home; and since we still were not stable enough financially to manage our own place, it was decided that, for a while at least, we would still live with them.

After a month-long search, we found a two-story house not far away. There was a living room, dining room, large kitchen, bath, and back porch downstairs and all the bedrooms, including a sitting room for Bob and me, upstairs.

As I would do with all the other places we lived, I committed to memory every inch of our new dwelling, fixing the positions of everything in my mind.

On a cold February day, with Bob behind me but letting me strictly alone, I walked into the still-empty house and through all the rooms, touching the walls, feeling where the doors and windows were, mentally measuring their widths.

I learned the locations of the stove, refrigerator, sink, cabinets, closets and how many shelves they contained. I counted the numbers of steps to the upstairs rooms, memorized the distances to the bedrooms, the sitting room, the bath.

If there were obstacles anywhere, I stored the knowledge in my personal memory bank. In less than fifteen minutes, I had visualized the entire layout. To this day, I can draw the floor plans of all the homes and apartments in which I lived during my blindness; they were, and still are, more vivid to me than if I had seen them.

After the furniture arrived, I did my memorizing routine again, coordinating what I learned with the layout: I committed to memory exactly where the living room couch was in relation to the door to the dining room; how many steps it took to reach any of the windows from the easy chairs; where the rocker stood, the length of the dining room table, the position of the chairs.

In the all-important upstairs area, I knew exactly how far the new baby's crib was from my bed. Soon the rooms and all they contained were fixed in my mind as though I carried a television screen inside my head.

After we moved in, our lives proceeded on an even keel.

Mother did the shopping, with me just helping. Before she left for her job, she would prepare as much of the evening meal as she could—a casserole, a meat dish, soup, a chicken. I would get the vegetables ready, pop things into the oven, set the table. I helped clean up, and I can say proudly that I never once dropped a dish. I also helped clean the house, running the vac and carpet sweeper, dusting, washing the bathroom and kitchen floors.

I took care of Stephanie—I'll explain how in a later chapter—and just kept getting bigger and bigger.

Julia picked the hottest day in my memory to make her entry into the world. On July 11, 1960, with the mercury soaring well over 100 degrees, I knew it was time to go to the hospital. I had anticipated a quick, easy delivery, but it proved to be neither for both of us.

I was in labor for eighteen hours, and for a while, it was touch and go whether my new baby would live.

Most babies are born head first, which is the easiest way because they can pass most readily through the fully dilated cervix and pelvic area. After the head emerges, the doctor turns it slightly so that the shoulders can also come easily through the birth canal.

But in my case, the doctor discovered a complication which is so rare that it occurs only in about one in 300 births. Somehow, the baby's neck had become twisted so that the head had entered the birth canal face first. The risk in this type of situation, known medically as a face or brow presentation, is that the head could wedge itself inside the pelvic region.

The abnormality can always be detected well in advance of actual labor so that steps to correct it can be taken. Some doctors may choose to perform a Caesarean section, feeling that taking the baby surgically is safer than trying to turn the baby, or performing what they call internal version. In my case, the doctor felt that the baby was in such a position that a combination of my own contractions, plus his own efforts to reach into the uterus and turn the baby, would be successful.

Despite sedation, the pain of the slow birth was agonizing.

"Now Charlotte," the doctor explained, "we can't give you too much of this stuff because it would weaken the uterine contractions, and we need all we can get." I winced and nodded.

"And besides," he continued, "too much of the painkiller can also cut down on the oxygen the baby receives and lead to troubles neither of us wants." I knew he was referring to breathing problems. I nodded again, then cried out as another spasm shot through me.

Finally, in the early hours of the morning, I obeyed the doctor's instruction to "bear down, Charlotte, bear down—just once more." The pain rose to a peak. I can remember that final moment when that last pain that gave my daughter existence swept through me. "Oh, God," I cried out. "I can't stand it. I'd rather die. My baby can't get here!"

And then blessed relief. The pain ended. The baby was born. I had another daughter.

But where was the cry, that first loud howl by which she announces her arrival into the world? I held my breath and listened, but it did not come.

Something was taking place behind the delivery table where I lay, my feet elevated in the stirrups, my arms secured at the table sides.

I heard a slap, and I knew the doctor was holding my baby upside down to remove mucus from the respiratory tract. The sound was like a dull dead thud. There was no response.

My heart began pounding, and I shut my eyes. My head

whirled, and I can remember weeping and uttering prayers.

Something was wrong. I heard the doctor call the nurses around him. I heard the scuffle of feet, and I sensed them working on my baby, trying to put life into her tiny body.

I remember thinking: "Was this to be my punishment because I had been so unhappy when I learned I was pregnant? Did I do this? Is it because I didn't think I could handle another baby? Oh God, forgive me." I knew as I lay there that if God would let her live, I could sustain that God-given life and help my baby grow.

Suddenly the cry came.

It wasn't loud but it seemed as though it filled the whole delivery room.

I lay exhausted but thankful. I knew they were cleaning up my baby now, weighing, measuring, placing drops in the eyes to prevent eye complications, all the required things. I heard more cries and then they brought my baby over to me and let me touch my beautiful daughter.

Chapter Eight

Bringing up my perfectly normal children presented some gigantic problems.

Even the simple act of feeding, no big deal for seeing mothers, had its difficulties, which I discovered to my chagrin the day I took my first baby home. Mother gave Stephanie her bottle for the noon feeding, but when I took over several hours later she howled with rage.

I was frightened. With the little vision I had left after Stephie was born, I peered closer and discovered she had turned her head and I had stuck the nipple into her ear. That evening it was worse. I jammed it up one nostril.

Finding the correct place where nipples ought to be inserted wasn't easy with squirmy babies whose mouths don't stay open and remain where they should, like little birds waiting for a worm. Every mother knows an infant darts and twists with lightning speed, and a mouth that was there and waiting one second is somewhere else the next. Until I figured out a way to beat her at this dodge-em game, poor Stephie's hair would practically be shampooed with formula which would also be dripping down the sides of her nose, her chin, and neck and saturating her kimonos and blankets. Stephie was probably the only baby I know who had to have her nightgowns changed more often than her diapers.

I finally solved the nipple-in-the-ear problem by holding on to the base of the rubber with two fingers while feeling with a third for the exact location of my baby's mouth.

I probably had the world's cleanest children. Since I was unable to tell if they had only spit up and messed their faces or just the tops of their nightgowns, I couldn't simply wash their mouths or hands or just change their gowns. To make sure, I just gave them a whole bath and changed all their clothes. I was washing them all the time. Those poor kids spent much of their infancy in the bathtub.

Looking back, it is easy to sound light-hearted, even a little flippant, about those first few years, and that's the way I want to remember them. But truth compels me to confess that when I was living through them, I felt no lightness, and flippancy was a stranger. Anxiety and anguish were a lot closer to me each day. I did a lot of praying those years, a lot of talking to God, and I must confess, a lot of crying too.

Stephanie slept in a cradle in our bedroom. Bob had given me an antique rocker for Christmas, and I used that when I fed her. I had dozens of cotton-knitted jackets which snapped in the front and covered her completely. They were easier for me to put on the baby than anything which would have to go over her head. I had them in all colors, prints and solids. While I always bathed my babies, dressed them, changed and cared for them, I did want somebody else to give any medicine that was prescribed to make sure much of the dose didn't dribble down their chins.

From the start, I used a large dining room table to clean and dress the babies. Our first one was set up just outside our bedroom. Wherever we moved, I had to have something like it—my changing table, I called it—a large area upon which everything I needed would be right at my fingertips: diapers, lotions, clothes for the day, everything organized and stacked in the same way. Other mothers used the tops of bassinets which they found useful in small areas, but I was not comfortable with such an arrangement. I didn't want to have to go across the room for something. My babies were bathed in a small plastic tub which I filled with a few inches of water and put on the table.

I kept the girls in playpens as long as I could, fearful of allowing them to roam unfettered—and unseen. Playpens are conveniences for both mothers and children because they are safe places for active youngsters and because the young child can sit, stand, or lie down as he or she wishes. But soon the time comes when the child demands greater freedom and squawls to emerge; some will find the playpen confining as early as nine months. For the most part, with a few exceptions, one of which could have ended in disaster, mine were reasonably content to remain awhile longer.

I had fully expected to take each of my children on my knee when I felt they could understand, and tell them, clearly and simply, that I was unable to see. Even when Stephie was still in the crawling stage, I found myself rehearsing what I would say. I must convey the knowledge, yet at the same time avoid frightening them or making them feel that they would be less protected.

It astonished me, but I never had to use the words. The children grew up understanding. They sensed almost from the beginning, before their developing powers of reasoning could tell them, that their mother was somehow different, and that remaining in the playpen was just one of the ways things had to be.

As they grew older, none would ever say things like, "Look, Mommy!" Instead, they would put objects into my hand. When Steph was only a few months old, she would take my hand and place it over a toy she wanted to show me. Somehow, she realized that was the way I "saw."

After they had left the playpen, they showed unmistakably that they knew. Most children leave their toys strewn around their rooms and play areas; instructions to pick them up and put them away usually go in one ear and out the other. My children, however, heeded—not because they were angels but because they understood why it was necessary, that I would trip if their things were left in the middle of the floor. From earliest years on they were always careful to lug their playthings out of my way after they had finished with them.

There was still another way my children seemed to know their mother could not see. All three learned to read unusually early. Bob and my parents read to them, and they continually interrupted with: "What's that letter?" and "make that sound." Before she was three, Stephanie was reading labels and even recipes on cans and boxes to me.

But if I have given you the notion that they were angels all the time, let me set the record straight quickly. For all their awareness of my handicap and despite all my extra vigilance, there were plenty of hair-raising experiences in our household. For a long time, I felt guilty about these, believing my blindness was to blame. Talks with our pastor convinced me, however, that they have happened—and unfortunately will continue to happen—to children with seeing parents too.

I don't think any mother with 20-20 vision could have prevented Julia from poking a bean up Stephie's nose. When Stephie howled and I managed to put together what had happened, I called Bob in a panic and he rushed home, stopping at a drugstore for a pair of tweezers. We held down the squirming Stephie and got the bean out.

Next day, Julia went one better. She stuck an inch-square wooden alphabet block deep into her sister's mouth, pushing it behind her teeth and twisting it. Hearing Stephanie's gurgles, I ran to her, felt her, and realized with a pounding heart what was there. But I kept my cool and was able to twist it out again. Why Stephie allowed Julia to feed her the block I'll never know.

Then there was the tea party. Will we ever forget that! It taught me a lesson some mothers must learn the hard way: to put poisonous substances out of reach of small children. Julia and Stephie had set their little table with their dishes and napkins, put out cookies, and were ready to serve tea. On other occasions, they had used soda pop or water, but this time one of them picked up a bottle of bleach and brought it to the table. Luckily, she diluted it with water before pouring some of the solution into the tea cups.

Apparently the taste was terrible because Stephie, the first to drink, began howling. I ran over and smelled the cup. Before rushing to the phone, I had the presence of mind to feel for Julia's cup and empty it in the sink. I dialed the operator and gave her my doctor's number, telling her it was an emergency. He told me to get Stephie to swallow milk and raw egg. She did, threw up, and that was the end of that.

While we were still living with Mom and Dad, Stephie gave Julia a lesson in how to get out of her playpen. Julia was only six months at the time, and was an adept pupil. Once or twice I caught her outside and, sighing, deposited her back in. One morning, while I was in the kitchen, she did her escape act, crawled into the bathroom, picked up a pair of my shoes, and happily tossed them into the toilet bowl.

After we moved into the new house, Julia continued to give me fits. One day, when she was about two, I found her in the bathroom holding the bottle of atropine drops I was using for my eyes. I yelled for Bob who came running. "My God," he said, "she must have drunk the stuff!"

Terrified, I called the doctor who barked into the phone: "Get her to the hospital at once. Two ounces of that medication taken internally could be lethal!"

I knew atropine caused blood vessels to swell. Julia could suffer a fatal hemorrhage.

I flew into her bedroom, grabbed a quilt, wrapped it around Julia and, with Bob helping me, dashed with her to the car. Tires screaming around corners, Bob raced to the hospital.

At the hospital, they pumped Julia's stomach. All they could do was watch her carefully for signs of hemorrhage. After a few hours, when nothing appeared, Bob went back home. In the bathroom he noticed a small puddle on the floor. He knelt to smell it. Then he put a drop on his finger and tasted it, which, he said later, was a pretty brave thing to do in a bathroom.

He called the hospital and spoke to the doctor, reporting what he found. It was the atropine, which Julia had simply poured out; she hadn't drunk a drop. Immensely relieved, we took her home. Bob said Julia was staring at both of us, probably wondering what the fuss was all about.

Just before we moved from Mom and Dad's house, Steph and Julia had just awakened from their morning naps. Steph was three and Julia a year and a half. I left them upstairs to play while I went downstairs to fix their lunch. I had just left the kitchen to bring them downstairs when I heard a loud thud outside the living room window.

I rushed upstairs and called out: "Stephanie, what was that? What was that terrible noise? Who's up here?"

In a voice about as emotional as though she was telling me the time, Stephanie replied: "Mommy, Julia just fell out the window."

My heart flip-flopped. I raced downstairs, bumping into our part-time cleaning lady. Together we rushed to the back of the house where Julia lay. There hadn't been any rain for weeks and the ground was rock-hard. She was whimpering. "Oh, God," I thought. "She's alive." But how badly had she been injured? We got a blanket and wrapped Julia in it, then I ran to the phone and telephoned for a taxi. It arrived in a few moments.

Carrying Julia, I told the driver: "Please hurry to the hospital. My little girl just fell out of a second-story window, and I think she's badly hurt." He stepped on the gas, and we fairly flew once again to the same hospital.

When the car stopped, I asked the driver: "Would you

please help me to the door? I'm blind." I heard a loud, "What?" He hadn't known. He leaped from the cab and rang the emergency button. In a few minutes, we had been taken inside, and the doctor was examining Julia.

By this time, my parents and Bob had come home for lunch. The cleaning lady had met them at the door and told them what had happened. Mother said she had never seen Bob drive so fast. They burst into the emergency room just as the doctor emerged with astounding news.

Not a bone in Julia's body was broken. She had landed on her hip, and the double diaper she wore had broken her fall. There were no internal injuries, either, and except for a sore hip, she escaped unscathed.

Back home, I learned what had happened. Steph and Julia had begun a game of "Superman" while they waited for their lunch. It was May, and their window was partly open. Julia had climbed on a cedar chest and, with Stephanie's complete approval, grabbed hold of the television aerial to "fly" down to the ground. Unfortunately, she was not superchild but just Julia Sanford, and she dropped like a stone.

Needless to say, these experiences taught me never to leave any bottles or containers of poisonous substances any place where children can reach them, and to make certain my children would never again be tempted to "fly" out of open windows.

As my family grew, Bob and the children would even play good-natured tricks on me. I'll never forget the glass-switching episode. I had set the table for dinner, knowing exactly where I was placing all the dinnerware, cutlery, and glasses. I had filled Bob's and the children's glasses with milk, which they drank by the gallon, and mine with water because from earliest days I never could stand the taste of milk. When dinner began, somebody quietly exchanged my water for a tumblerful of milk. I reached for it, took a deep swallow, and ran for the sink. Everyone guffawed, and so did I when I returned.

Then there was the case of the bug lunch. I fixed some macaroni and cheese for the children and me. It tasted perfectly fine, and we all ate with relish. I wrapped the leftovers in foil and put them back in the refrigerator.

That evening, instead of mashed potatoes, I decided we'd have the macaroni and cheese as a side dish. Thrifty Charlotte. When we sat down to dinner, I heard Bob's astonished voice. "Did you three have this for lunch?" he asked. The children, mouths full, mumbled something, and I said: "Sure, it's really good, honey. Go ahead and try it."

Indignantly: "I will not. It's got bugs in it!"

I know that my stomach did a flip-flop, and I'm sure I must have turned pale. "Yep," Bob repeated, obviously staring into his plate. "Nice little dead bugs, spicing up the cheese." The girls, who had certainly seen the little dark things, thought they were pepper. In a moment my stomach righted itself, and I managed a weak joke. "Go ahead," I said. "It's just some extra protein." The stuff got scraped into the garbage can, but we were able to laugh about it because nobody was hurt. If Brazilians can eat white ants and the Chinese consider grasshoppers a delicacy, we could ingest a little sprinkling of tiny whatever-they-were without too much damage.

Mommy was the butt of jokes such as this—none of course done meanly or intended to hurt. Everybody seemed to understand that they created a crucial atmosphere of lightness. Life can become very heavy in a home with a handicapped mother.

Many people wondered if I watched television. I certainly did! From the very beginning, I would sit with Bob and the children as they grew, "watching" with them, listening to the words and allowing my imagination to create the accompanying scenes. When the screen lapsed into total silence, Bob explained in a few words what was happening.

And movies? I adored them and not for a moment did I stop going. I know people were amazed when Bob and I told them we were on our way to a show, or had seen a new Elizabeth Taylor, Pat Boone, or Elvis Presley film that month. I didn't miss much. "The mind has a thousand eyes," wrote the British poet Francis William Bourdillon. I know that I "saw" more with my mind than most people whose vision was limited to the pictures that flickered before them.

Chapter Nine

While we were still living with my parents, I had noticed that Bob had been preoccupied for weeks. He seemed distant; often I had to ask a question several times before he answered.

One evening, in pillow talk, I finally learned what was troubling him. Bob wasn't moving ahead in business as rapidly as he wanted, and he felt he had hit upon the reason.

"A college degree isn't a surefire passport to success," he told me, "but it's tough to get ahead without one. Oh sure, guys have done it and always will; but you can't underestimate the importance of those credentials."

He paused. A rustle of bedclothes came to my ears. I knew he had clasped his hands around his head and was staring at the ceiling. Bob, I knew, had not returned to school for his final year after the army.

"What's the problem?" I asked lightly, turning toward him, though I realized at once with a sinking heart that the problem, like all Gaul, was divided into three parts, two babies and me. It had not occurred to me until that moment that Bob wanted—and surely needed—to complete his education, but once I knew, I could not stand in his way even though it meant loneliness, separation, and perhaps even hardship for a whole year.

"Look," I said, moving closer, feeling his warmth. I reached for his hand, and he lowered it from his head to grasp mine. "I have my folks here. Mother will not only be company but will help me with the babies. And you know

Dad; he just can't be around them enough. If I don't stop him, he'll be spoiling them rotten with attention.

"We'll be just fine. And K.S.U. isn't all that far away, just a few hundred miles. I can come up to visit you, and you'll be coming home to visit us. We've had worse problems." I was pretending a cheerfulness I did not feel.

He loosed my hand, rose, and paced the floor. I knew he was struggling with a critical decision. "The kids," he said, half to himself. "Can I leave them now? Can I leave you?" There was a fourth problem neither of us had mentioned: we had very little money.

I read his thoughts. "The babies and I will be fine," I said firmly, sitting up in bed and turning my head to follow his footsteps. "We can borrow the money for expenses, and you'll probably be able to get your part-time job back at the shoe store where you worked as an undergrad. Did you forget that the owner thought you were one of the best salesmen he ever had and practically said there'd be a job whenever you wanted it?

"Yep," I chirruped gaily, "I think it's a grand idea." I added the sensible point that if he was going to do it at all, this was really the best time, before we moved into our own place, where there would be nobody to help me. Having planted this argument, I turned on the happy talk again to convince him that I was solidly behind his decision.

"Imagine," I rattled on, "a college grad. Let's see, where will we hang the diploma? How about the john?"

He laughed, came back to the bed, and his arms crept around me. "Are you sure?" he asked.

"I'm very sure," I answered. "About everything but the diploma in the john."

I reached toward him, and his arms tightened. I felt his lips on mine.

Bob left soon after and, married less than three years, we were apart again.

It was unbearably lonely without him. I busied myself

97

with the children and the house, wrote him many letters, and waited for his replies. He was staying at his old fraternity house, the Farmhouse, and had indeed gotten back his job at the shoe store. He'd telephone home every Wednesday evening, and I'd make sure nobody used the phone after dinner until his call came.

"That child acts like a lovesick teenager waiting for a call from her boyfriend," I heard Mother tell Dad one evening.

Unhappiness comes in clumps.

That year, Dad became seriously ill. His handsome face had taken on a scary grayness; he tired easily, and his breathing would often sound unnatural. He entered the hospital for a series of tests, but the doctors could not pinpoint the cause.

He returned home, less and less able to work with his customary vitality, yet cheerful as ever. The burden now fell on Mother and me with an increasing heaviness. Bob wanted to leave the university and come back home, but I wouldn't hear of it.

"We will manage," I told him. "God will provide."

I did not feel the optimism I had put into my voice. God does indeed provide, but in His own time and in His own way. And sometimes the trials we must undergo can be harsh.

With Dad out of work most of the time and medical bills piling up, we plunged into a severe money pinch. Mother's salary was barely enough to cover our needs. I never let Bob know how badly off we really were. I know that no matter what I said, he would have given up his chance for a college degree, most likely for good.

But there was no way I could hide our plight from our close friends.

One day, a letter arrived. "This is a funny one," Mother

observed as she picked it out from the batch of circulars, store ads, and other junk mail. "It has no return address." I heard the sound of tearing as she ripped open the envelope.

"Here," she said, "what's this?" She told me a piece of paper had fluttered to the floor. It was a cashier's check for sixty dollars.

She read me the letter that accompanied it. "We want to help you and Bob," it said, "because we know you both and love you both. . . ." A check for the same amount would come each month, the letter continued, until the bad times passed, and Bob and I could get back on a stable financial footing. Our benefactors did not want to be repaid.

There was no signature.

God shows his love for us through people.

Spring came early that year. By late February, Mother was telling me that the crocuses were open and the daffodils were already lifting their curved heads. Daffodils had always been a sign of hope and rebirth for me, the promise of a new beginning. With the opening of the fat buds, nature is reminding us that the season of new life for all things is starting anew.

Soon Bob came home. He was now a college graduate, and it did seem that at least some of the dark clouds were lifting at last. There was a joyous reunion, a bountiful coming-home dinner and—before too long—Bob landed a new job. There was a drawback, but we pushed it aside. He was hired by a grain inspection company to check grain elevators and storage facilities in the Kansas, Missouri, and Oklahoma area, and was provided with an automobile for his trips.

Once again, I lived for the days he would come home; this time, he was able to make it every weekend. If ever I needed proof that I loved Bob, that year of separation, followed by those weeks of traveling for his new job, gave it to me. For I missed him terribly, missed his voice, his jovial presence, his concern. "Oh Lord," I whispered during the lonely evenings before drifting to sleep, "I know I can never live without him."

I had been aware for some time that, sooner or later, we would have to leave the security of my parents' home and strike out on our own. It would be a giant step, I knew, but I had to face the reality of my position: Mother and Dad would not be a refuge forever, and I had to become totally self-sufficient as a blind mother.

Bob and I talked things over and decided this had to be the time. He would look for a job that would keep him in Coffeyville and, weekends, we would search for a house. In no time at all, we found both.

Bob landed a good job as manager of a men's clothing store in town, and soon after we stumbled upon a house at the end of Spruce Street that met all our requirements. It had a huge screened-in porch which ran all across the front, deep enough for the girls to ride their tricycles out there and keep their doll buggies, little tables and chairs, and assorted other toys. I could simply hook the screen door and know they would be safe. The backyard was large and completely fenced-in.

I was excited and at the same time apprehensive. For the first time we were going to live by ourselves as a family. But I wouldn't have Mother to do most of the cooking. Had I learned enough to do it alone?

Before we moved in, I did my usual memorizing act. Then I went back home and planned every detail of the furnishing and decorating, working it all out on that screen in my mind. Before long, I knew exactly where everything would go. And more: I knew what colors I wanted the various rooms painted.

I know that sounds surprising: people can be forgiven for wondering what on earth difference colors would make to a blind woman. The living room could be purple with red and yellow polka dots for all she'd know.

That's just the point. I *would* know, and I cared. Blind persons who once knew colors remember them very clearly. So even though I would never really see them, clashing colors would bother me no end.

I could hear the astonishment in the boss painter's voice when I marched through the house, telling him I wanted a certain shade of beige but to be careful not to make it too yellow or too pink; and that I wanted a cheerful white here but not too starkly so; that the green there must be subdued, not shout.

In the bedroom, I told him, the walls must be maroon. By this time, the boss painter had apparently completely forgotten my blindness.

"Say," he said, "don't you think that's too dark? Waking up in the morning and seeing a dark red, won't that be depressing? You want to look at something brighter, don't you?"

I explained that I had a maroon figured rug and I wanted the walls to pick up that color. "But don't you worry about the brightness," I told him. "We'll have white drapes and a white bedspread for contrast."

It was all done precisely as I wanted, and friends who saw it exclaimed delightedly that the house looked lovely. I glowed with pride.

We set up a system for marketing. On weekends, Bob would drive me to the supermarket, but I would do my shopping, with some minor help from Bob.

Supermarkets always stock their merchandise in the same places, and once I knew the aisles and what they contained, choosing the foods wasn't all that difficult. Who can't tell a chicken from hamburger meat? I also kept up with the prices of foods by conferring often with Mother and would pass up items I felt were too costly that week. I chose the fruits and vegetables I wanted, and thanks to my acute sense of smell, rarely brought home an unripe melon.

Back home, I placed all the provisions in precise positions on the pantry shelves which allowed me to get whatever I needed without asking anyone. I had an electric stove installed so that I could turn the burners to the correct heat by pressing buttons and turning dials instead of igniting a gas flame, which would be trickier to handle.

I had little trouble fixing meals. I broiled steaks, chops, and hamburgers, using my sense of smell to determine the degree of doneness. After a while my nose became so expert that I could prepare a steak or roast to exact specifications— medium, medium-well, or whatever. Fried chicken, roast turkey? Again, my nose—plus a jab with a fork—told me when they were ready.

Nobody complained and certainly nobody starved, so I started to go to town. I used to make spaghetti with prepared sauces, but now I began to concoct my own. Bob was amazed when he came home one late afternoon to the delicious aroma of tomato sauce, Italian tomatoes, onion, garlic, oregano, basil, and a few other ingredients simmering in a large pot on the stove. He was dumbfounded when I asked him to get me a gourmet cookbook; but he did, and on special occasions I put together a meal that drew sighs of satisfaction from him.

Elated by my successes, I began experimenting with baking, and before long I was turning out cakes and pies, some from scratch. I had a set of measuring spoons, the kind that linked together on a ring, and could easily tell the size I needed by feel. The measuring cups were marked on the outside by raised numbers that told me where the quarter-cup, half-cup, and full-cup levels were. My children and Bob read the recipes, and I went to work, mixing, kneading, pouring, and shoving into the oven. Everything turned out fine.

I did my own ironing with a regular iron and ironing board. I did my own mopping of floors, a chore I never liked because I had to get on my hands and knees to feel the floors. I did my own laundry and folded clothes by feel.

Everything was getting done, and done well. But it took a toll.

If anything I've written gives anyone the notion that I was a kind of wonder woman zipping through a normal life despite my blindness, forget it.

For one thing, there was never an untired bone in my body. Bringing up babies was the most exhausting work I had ever done in my life.

For another, in all the years of my blindness I was almost never on time for anything except meals, and even those were late more often than I wanted them to be. Whenever we went anywhere—the movies, church, a club metting, or wherever—Bob would be ready long before I was.

I can't count the times he would holler up to me: "Charlotte! It's getting *late!* Can't you get a move on?"

And the times I'd answer: "Just one more second, honey, I'm coming right down."

There was so much to do and so little time. Before dressing, I'd have to make certain the house was in order. Unable to look around and pick up the shoes and the magazines, I had to feel for order with my hands and feet, feel the floors by shuffling across every inch, feel the beds, the bureau tops, the tables, chairs, everything in the room. I spent more time feeling than most women do cleaning and dusting. When I found something, it had to be put in its assigned place, or it would be lost a long time. The children's undershirts, panties, shoes, jackets had to be folded and carefully put where they belonged, like the parts of a motor. Things that matched couldn't be separated, or Stephie would go around next day in a ludicrous outfit, and don't think that some days she and Julia didn't! Once Julia happily played around the house with two left shoes, though incidents like those were happily few.

Then, before I'd be able to leave with a clear mind, I'd have to give some more suggestions to an already over-instructed baby-sitter, ask the children one more time if there was something they wanted before we left, and, of course, make sure I looked okay. Curiously, I would find myself moving toward a mirror after dressing, even though I could no longer view the image reflected back. It was a strange reversion to the times when I had vision. I would feel my hair, run my fingers down the front and sides of my dress, feel the hem.

That was important to me. I had to look as though I had just stepped out of a bandbox. Spotless. Perfect. Nobody must feel sorry for me or pity for Bob.

Chapter Ten

Like shifting clouds on a day that can't make up its mind what it wants to be, my life alternated between brightness and gloom. The joy I felt at being able to manage and make a life was now dimmed by the chilling news that Daddy needed open-heart surgery.

His illness had finally been diagnosed as endocarditis, a disease of the valves that control the blood flow through the heart.

The doctor explained to me what had happened:

"Many years ago," he said, "your Dad had had an attack of rheumatic fever but never knew it. It's not easy to recognize and diagnose even now, and certainly it was difficult then. As a result, some of his heart muscle and an important valve had become scarred. The valve is kind of like a one-way swinging door, allowing blood to flow out of a chamber of the heart and through the body but preventing the blood from flowing back in. The valve just doesn't work well any more, and blood keeps leaking back into the chamber from which it came. This blood keeps backing up there, impeding the normal flow, and bringing about a congestion. As a result, the whole circulatory system has become sluggish. That's why your father is constantly short of breath, gets tired easily, and always looks so pale."

The diseased valve, he said, must be replaced with a plastic one or Daddy might not survive for too long.

These days, open-heart surgery is well advanced, almost routine. But back in 1962, the technique of cutting into the human heart while the blood flow is rerouted away from it by a heart-lung machine was little more than a decade old. It was very risky business.

But it had to be done to give Daddy a chance to live. So just a few months after we had moved into our own home, we took him to the Kansas University Medical Center.

How does anybody describe the hours in a hospital waiting room while a loved one is undergoing a life-or-death operation? Mother and I sat on a bench with my father's older brother, Dwight. We said little. I prayed most of the time.

Sitting there in my darkness, my mind went back over the years, as though turning the pages of a treasured family album. I remembered the time he had sat with me all night long during a violent wind and thunderstorm, calming my terrors. I remembered being held in his strong arms as a child and comforted when I had tripped and painfully hurt my leg. I remembered especially the night he came to my room just before I went away to college. "I just want to say good-by to my girl," he had said. His voice was quivering. I had felt his face, and it was wet with tears.

The operation began at eight in the morning. The surgeon had told us it would probably take about seven hours, but at noon Mother saw him approaching us. "My God!" she cried. We all bolted upright. Had something happened to Daddy?

The surgeon quickly reassured us. "It went more quickly than we had anticipated," he said. "We've done all we can. He's in the recovery room now, and you will be able to see him in about an hour."

Dad recovered from the surgery but could never again work at his old job. All he was able to do was take on part-time work that did not require much physical activity. The doctor told him to walk as much as possible, and that was fine because we lived eight blocks away and he was able to come over frequently to play with my daughters.

From inside, I could tell when he was arriving because the girls would be peering out the window and, at the first glimpse of him, set up a clamor that shook the house. Their excitement was doubtless due to the fact that Grandpa's coming meant gorging on candy and ice cream bars from the little grocery nearby, treats I knew were bad for their appetites and worse for their teeth—but great for Grandpa's spirit as well as theirs.

Well, I reasoned, dentists can always fill cavities, but who can put glorious memories of a loving grandfather into the minds of children? And who can replace a grandfather who so obviously enjoyed his hours with his grandchildren? I have seen so many young parents who, with set ideas about bringing up children, almost literally elbow aside grandparents eager to help. "You'll spoil them rotten!" "We don't do that in our house!" "That's bad for their psyches!" Sound familiar? Young fathers and mothers who bark these and other no-no's at their parents, who consider them old-fashioned and meddling, should understand that some of the most treasured thoughts children can ever have, memories that will endure for a lifetime, will be those of their grandparents. And that, second only to the joy of having their own children, is the happiness of grandchildren.

My children were growing up, and soon it was time for Stephanie to start school. She was wildly excited while I dreaded this next step and the adjustments that we'd have to make.

Most mothers would walk their little kindergartners to school, but I couldn't, and Bob and I were apprehensive about letting Stephie go by herself. The Garfield School, which she would attend, was nine blocks away, and there were broad streets with traffic to cross.

There was one out: move. So we did. Early in 1964, we found a home right across from the kindergarten door, a small house with two bedrooms, a tiny utility room we used as a playroom for the girls, and a covered patio off the kitchen. There was no fenced-in yard or screened front porch, but by this time Julia was almost four and completely aware that I couldn't see. Although she was as active a little girl as any I've ever known, she knew that she could not stray from home. I had complete confidence that she would not.

The new house was very clean and had been completely redecorated throughout, with brand-new gold shag carpeting and off-white wallpaper with gold designs in the bedrooms. The kitchen had half windows on three sides, and Mother had run up some white dotted Swiss curtains for them. It had a bright, cheerful kitchen, sunny much of the day.

Please glance back at the preceding paragraph, then ask yourself if you haven't done so already: "How on earth could a blind woman know all that?"

Oh, I did, all right! I asked detailed questions about every aspect of the house, felt the floors, the curtains, the painted walls and woodwork, smelled—yes, *smelled!*—the cleanliness, and felt the warmth of the sun in the kitchen. Knowing and feeling all this, it was easy to imagine all the rest.

Years before, my home teacher had given me a long white cane. I had used it only a few times. On Stephie's first day at school, I fished it out of the closet and waited outside for Marilyn Lively and her daughter Lori to come along. The Livelys, good friends, lived close, and it would be Lori's first day too. Marilyn was going to help me into the school and show me the way if I ever had to go by myself.

The four of us set out on our short walk. I took the cane for a special reason. I wanted the other children to see it and know from the first day that Stephie's mother was blind. I thought if the truth was out at once, openly, Stephie's classmates would take my blindness routinely and accept it. There would be no risk that it would be discovered by chance, whispered around the class, and then, with the cruelty that children can exhibit at times, be used to torment Stephanie.

Well, I reckoned dead wrong.

Not only did I misread children's common sense and human understanding, but I got a good lesson from Stephie herself.

Just as we got to the schoolroom door, Stephie tugged at my arm and said loudly: "Mommy, I wish you wouldn't carry that cane." I thought at once: "She's ashamed to let her classmates know that her mother was different." She wasn't at all.

"Mommy," she said, matter-of-factly, "I'm really afraid that when you wave it like that, you're going to poke one of the children in the tummy with it."

I hid the cane as best I could that day and, when I got back home, threw it back into the closet and never used it again.

As for the classmates, never at any time or at any age did they taunt any of my children because their mother could not see. Yes, I know, and other mothers will agree, that children can sometimes be cruel to their friends; but my own experiences have shown that they can be more tolerant, more truly accepting of things as they are than many grownups. Children are reasonable and above all fair —"very receptive to elementary ideas of justice," the famous Dr. Arnold Gesell of Yale University has written.

Our children are finer human beings than most of us realize, and I would like to talk more about this.

In William Wordsworth's great poem, *Ode: Intimations of Immortality,* he suggests that, because of the "dream-like vividness and splendor" with which children first see things around them, we almost all have had a previous state of existence. In a beautiful passage, he writes:

Our birth is but a sleep and a forgetting;
The Soul that rises with us, our life's Star,

Hath had elsewhere its setting
And cometh from afar;
Not in entire forgetfulness,
And not in entire nakedness,
But trailing clouds of glory do we come
From God, who is our home . . .

The Soul, from God's nearness, enters a child's body
when it is born. While the child is still young—while he or
she is still "a six years' darling of a pigmy size"—the bliss
of that earlier existence is still remembered. Heaven "lies
about us in our infancy." Mothers who cuddle their new-
born babies and pour out their love for them, I believe,
feel this nearness to God. And I believe, too, that children's
essential humanity to children stems from their instinctive
realization that they are all still newly arrived "from afar."
Man's later inhumanity to man, sadly, comes because, as
Wordsworth says, the passing years "bring the inevitable
yoke."

Yet we are not lost as society's pressure weighs upon
us. There are times during pauses in our madly rushing
lives when our bright and shiny souls can recall their
origins, when they "have sight of that immortal sea/Which
brought us hither." And, when life ends, our souls can, in
one moment of time, travel back from whence they came,
back to the glories they once knew, back to the nearness
with God.

I needn't have had any qualms about her classmates'
attitude toward Stephie. Almost from that first day on, they
were around the house a great deal, and the gangs got
larger as she progressed through school. Only they weren't
coming to have make-believe tea parties or play with dolls.
They wanted Stephie to come out and play first base.

There's another curious fact I discovered about my

children. While they reacted to my blindness in a very special way, as I pointed out earlier, they also developed along their own paths as human beings in their own right. Stephie, from the beginning, was a tomboy. If she couldn't care less about stuffed toys, she sure could slam out a three-bagger or carry a football across a goal line. Julia, on the other hand, was wild about her ballet and tap lessons, and had a whole roomful of dolls she played with constantly.

Shifting clouds.

We had been settled in the new house for less than a year when Bob became increasingly dissatisfied with his job and began searching for a new one. One day in the early summer of 1965, an offer came from a high-fashion men's store. More pay, a better establishment, and a good chance to move ahead. There was a catch—it was in Emporia, Kansas, about 150 miles away.

For days we played the game of "should we, shouldn't we?" I shrank from the thought of moving again, especially from the city where I was born, where my family lived, where we had so many friends. Oh, the children could adjust; they were young and flexible. But could I? How quickly? And what about the people? Would they be thoughtful, friendly, kind? Or strange and hostile?

Even though Bob at first insisted it would be better to remain in Coffeyville, I felt I had no right to stand in his way if the chances for advancement were measurably better. After all, I said to him quite sensibly, the entire family would benefit by Bob's improving circumstances.

So the decision was made. We would move to Emporia.

But then came the mumps.

Julia caught it first from one of her partners in the chorus line while rehearsing for the dance recital. Julia gave it to Stephanie, and we nursed her through the ordeal. Neither Bob nor I was worried about ourselves because we both had gone through the disease years before and felt we were at least partly immune. Both of us, we remembered, had had the swelling only on one side, but wasn't that good enough?

It wasn't. After Stephie came me. And after me, Bob.

There we were, all four of us with cheeks like chipmunks, feverish, heads pounding, and jaws aching painfully from the swelling.

The two girls and I hurt just from the neck up, but in men and boys past puberty, mumps can spread to the testicles. Since years have passed I can look back upon that time with some wry humor, though it was anything but funny at the time.

It hurt, Bob said, like the very hammers of hell.

"Better get him to the hospital," the doctor said, so we called an ambulance. It arrived promptly enough, but one of the two men who came with the stretcher took a quick look at Bob's swollen jaw and made for the door, calling as he fled:

"I ain't gonna carry him. I never had the mumps myself!"

Daddy volunteered to help and, though he wasn't supposed to bear heavy loads, held up one end as Bob was placed in the ambulance.

"That hospital was only two miles away," Bob told me later, "yet I can swear that the driver hit every bump on the way. If he managed to miss any, he probably backed up and made for it. That's not all. The ambulance had a faulty exhaust system, and the fumes were seeping into the interior from a hole in the tailpipe. I didn't know what would get me first, asphyxiation or the agony of the next bump."

At the hospital, whoever decides such things said Bob had to be put into isolation. Fine. He preferred that, sighing: "I want to be miserable all by myself." Unfortunately, the hospital's only isolation room was in the basement. It also doubled as a heavily guarded security room for criminals.

It had no telephone, and the curtainless windows were barred. There was no air conditioning. Moreover, the room faced east, and the hot July sun poured through the windows all day long. Poor Bob lay sweltering in bed with a high fever, his swollen face looking, he said later, like a basketball, and everything hurting. I couldn't visit him because I was too miserable myself, and his only callers during that week-long bout were the doctor and nurses.

Finally his fever broke, the swellings went down, and he recovered with no ill effects. So did we all, and our thoughts turned to the Big Move.

Bob and I drove up to Emporia, feeling good now about the adventure ahead. We sang as we drove up Route 169, past the broad pasture lands of the Bluestem Belt, named for the color of the grasses that bend to the winds of that region of the country which forms part of the great plains.

Soon we were on the outskirts of Emporia, home of William Allen White, one of America's most famous editors. From his office at 517 Market Street, Mr. White produced his Emporia *Gazette* which earned international fame for him and his town. Mr. White was succeeded in his editorial chair by his son, W. L. White, who became equally well-known. We drove past Peter Pan Park where we saw children playing and wading in the pool presented to the city by the White family, and stopped to look at the bust of William Allen White, created by the sculptor Jo Davidson.

Emporia was a small city then, with a population of barely 16,000, and hasn't grown a great deal since. The seat of Lyon County, it sits squarely in the middle of farming and dairy country. Bob described it to me as a lovely place, and my spirits soared even higher.

We spent a few days house-hunting and found a place for rent on Walnut Street, four blocks from a school and not all that far from shopping. It was tiny—a living room, two bedrooms, kitchen, and bath—but we felt it would do nicely, especially since it had a fair-sized backyard. Once again, the utility room would be converted, Sanford-style, into a playroom.

We returned to Coffeyville, and the job of packing was begun.

It was no easy matter. By that time, we had collected, as all families will, a vast quantity of personal possessions, certainly not excluding the children's belongings which seemed to be increasing by the week and were already spilling all over the place. Trying to get them to part with anything was a little like asking the Queen of England which of her crown jewels she would choose to do without.

I insisted that everything had to be labeled and crated so that on our arrival in Emporia the contents could be placed in the exact positions I wanted them. It took a long time but at last it was finished.

From deep inside the house, where I was shuffling my feet and feeling for anything we might have left behind, I heard the van's big engine start and the gears clash as it started up the street. A squeal of brakes, and it was turning at the corner, heading toward our new home. Not long after, Mother and I, with the two girls, piled into Dad's car, and we too set off. Bob had gone on ahead.

Shifting clouds.

There was sunshine again. Because on our arrival in Emporia my fears about our Big Move were washed away in the flood of kindness shown to us.

I will never accept the conviction, held as an article of faith by so many, that people are cold and unfriendly, that human beings are essentially self-centered creatures. that man's inhumanity to man is the central theme of our times, and that, as one recent so-called "self-help" book put it, we must look out for "No. 1." I believe that the indifference many people seem to have for others is only a thin shell, a veneer worn only because they are fearful of being hurt, of not being accepted by others. Beneath that thin shell is love and the need for love.

Certainly it is true that "No. 1" is important—all human beings must direct their thoughts and actions inward toward their own welfare. But there is also a "No. 2," or let me say a "No. 1-A" because it is coequal. And that is the group or the other person. Our civilization would never have been able to develop and flourish if all members of society were not also just as deeply concerned about the group's welfare. For once the health and safety of the group withers and begins to die, can the individual have any hope of surviving alone?

Each of us, knowingly or not, contributes to other people's lives. The happiest are those who are aware that they do, who are honest enough, unafraid enough to unbend and tell others: "We care."

The people of Emporia where we went to live cared and showed it. Perhaps the spirit of William Allen White permeated the neighborhood and the town itself. When Mr. White presented the city with a large tract of land where the park was eventually created, he said that in each dollar bill there lay three "kicks." The first, he explained, is when one earns it, the second when one is thrifty enough to save it. And the third? "When you give it away," said Mr. White. "And that is the biggest one of all."

We had barely arrived at our new house, beating the slower moving van with our furniture, when two women— bless them both—who lived across the street knocked on our door, bearing armfuls of food. "We thought you'd all be hungry after your long ride," one of them explained. That evening, knowing that we would hardly be ready to cook dinner, a neighbor came with heaps of fried chicken, large sliced tomatoes, and a mouth-watering chocolate cake covered with white icing.

They, and our other neighbors, were telling us they cared. For all the time we lived in Emporia, we found friendliness, and we found love in the true Biblical sense.

Getting settled was just as hectic as it always had been, but finally we finished the job. We bade a tearful good-by to Mother and Dad and began our new lives. Bob went to work for a men's store, Stephie started school in the fall, and I kept house.

Shifting clouds, darkening with illness.
Julia developed a cold which she couldn't shake. And I felt pretty sick myself—my head ached, I had pains in the arms and legs and spells of dizziness. Bob decided the two of us needed a doctor.

After we got Stephanie off to school, Bob took Julia and me to the doctor's office. I went in first, and he looked at my throat, listened to my chest with a stethoscope, and said I had the flu. "Go to bed, if you can, Mrs. Sanford," he advised, "take aspirin and lots of liquids. Now let's look at your daughter."

As he examined and questioned Julia, I could hear the concern in his voice. I reached out for Bob's hand, and he held mine very tight. Then the doctor said, "I'm afraid she's a pretty sick girl. I want her in the hospital immediately." Julia, he said, had a bacterial pneumonia.

We took her right to the hospital where she stayed for eleven days. She turned out to be allergic to penicillin, so the doctor used other less powerful drugs; and it took Julia a long time to get over the pneumonia and even longer to get back her strength.

Mother and Dad came to Emporia for the Thanksgiving holiday, and I could sense that something was wrong. Dad slept a lot and had even less energy than he had after his surgery. Bob and I tried to persuade the folks to move to Emporia. We sat around the dinner table talking, and Bob told Dad: "Why not? You would be able to come and spoil the girls every afternoon again.

"I'm sure I can help you get a job here," he assured

Dad. But Dad wouldn't hear of any such plan. I thought he was probably just having a bad week. Actually, he was more gravely ill than any of us suspected.

A few weeks later, on December 10, they stopped in Emporia again. Uncle Harold and Aunt Rubye Rauch were with them, and we celebrated Mother's birthday that day. The festivities were somewhat low-key because they were on their way to the Kansas City Medical Center. Dad didn't feel well, and although the doctors thought he had the flu, the usual medicines were not helping. So it was decided that he should return to the medical center. Mother stayed in Kansas City with him.

Both girls came down with chicken pox, first Stephanie who doubtless picked it up from one of her classmates, and then Julia, still weak after her bout with pneumonia and susceptible to any bug in the neighborhood. Fortunately, they weren't too sick, but I was kept very busy with the calamine lotion and the effort to keep them in bed.

So although it hurt me a great deal, I wasn't able to visit Daddy who was still at the medical center. On Christmas Eve, Mother came down from Kansas City and went with Bob and me across the street to our neighbors for dinner. The girls were still not allowed out, and Bob's parents, who were visiting from Coffeyville, had dinner with them.

The next day was Christmas. Mother and I, carrying brightly wrapped gifts, got on the train for Kansas City to spend the day with my father. When we walked into his room, I heard his voice, once so strong and hearty, in a whispered greeting. I knew at once he had grown much weaker.

Mother put the presents on his bed and helped him open them. I heard the rustle of paper and his exclamations of delight, whispered not boomed out as in years gone by. After a few minutes, he asked suddenly: "Say, have you had lunch?"

117

We said we had not, though it was almost midday.

"Well then, let's all go down to the cafeteria," he told us, his voice now a little stronger. I bit my lip. Christmas dinner in a hospital cafeteria.

We helped him into a wheelchair and pushed him downstairs to the square, bare-walled lunchroom. I had a ham salad sandwich, some cranberry salad, and a soft drink, all that was left. We sat at a corner table and talked for more than an hour. I rattled on about Stephie and Julia, and Daddy laughed softly at some of the antics I described. It was probably the most memorable Christmas dinner I've ever had, one I'll never forget, because it was the last one Mother, Daddy, and I spent together.

On the way back to his room, I linked my arm into Mother's as she pushed Dad in his wheelchair. Dad insisted on holding my unfinished drink, but he couldn't keep it steady, and he spilled it over himself. "I'm sorry," he whispered.

Upstairs, back in his bed, he said to us: "You'd better call the nurse." I heard his breathing, short, labored. The nurse came and gave him an injection. "Thank you, ma'am," Dad said to her. His breathing eased, and he slept.

Daddy slept most of the afternoon, and Mother and I alternated between standing in the corridor, talking with the nurses and other visitors, and sitting beside his bed listening to his labored breathing. It was hard for me to leave. Although we didn't voice it and maybe wouldn't admit it even to ourselves, it was obvious that he was getting weaker.

Finally, Mother took me back to Emporia and immediately caught the next train back to Kansas City. I went to bed, virtually exhausted, and woke up the next morning, itching all over.

Bob took one look at me and burst out laughing. "Charlotte," he said, between guffaws, "I'm sorry but you look so funny. You're covered with red spots." I had the chicken pox. Well, unlike my daughters, I felt awful. I didn't sleep for three nights because of the itching. Once, when Bob was smoothing the calamine lotion on my shoulders, he decided to count the pox.

"One, two, three," he counted and went on and on and on. He said he was halfway between my shoulders and waist when he got tired of counting—at 2,001.

Mother called from Kansas City every few hours, telling us what was being done for Daddy. He was getting weaker and had signed consent forms agreeing to experimental treatments. "If I can help anyone else, do what you have to do," he said to his doctor. He lay in bed, hooked up to all kinds of tubes and apparatus, whispering to Mom when she was allowed in for five minutes every hour.

Years before, when the doctor had first diagnosed his bad heart, he had been warned to "quit smoking for your own good." Of course he never did until these weeks, and he retained the humor and sense of mischief I will always remember.

On one of her five-minute visits, Dad motioned to Mother to bend down. She leaned over, her ear close to his mouth, and heard him say, "You know, I was thinking something funny, Gerry. I've finally quit smoking, and it's killing me." He wasn't laughing at death, of course, but trying to make it easier for Mother.

The last time she was allowed into his room, Mother told us that Dad, with desperate last-minute strength, pulled her down, kissed her, and told her he loved her. Then he said, "Take care of all my babies." He was speaking of Stephanie, Julia, and me at the end, which came on January 6, 1966.

After Dad's death, Mother went back to Coffeyville and quickly made arrangements to move to Emporia so she could be near us. She got a job as housemother for the boys' dormitory at the College of Emporia, a Presbyterian school. Having been close only to girls, first me and then Stephanie and Julia, she adored the antics of "her boys."

Then it was time for Julia to enter kindergarten. She was a tiny little thing, with big, brown eyes and a long ponytail that I brushed every morning. She had a collection of about twenty stuffed lambs that she loved dearly, and each night when I went to hear her prayers and tuck her in, she would sit solemnly and insist that I say goodnight to each of her "lambies."

The day before school was to begin, Bob and I drove her along the path she would take, Bob carefully pointing out landmarks for her to follow. We followed that up by walking with her along the same route to familiarize her with it.

The next morning, Julia selected her clothes carefully. She picked out a pink dotted Swiss dress and painstakingly tied a bow around her favorite lamb's neck because she had decided that it must go to school too.

At the last minute, I had some qualms, and I wanted to go with her but Bob said, "She's big enough, she can go all by herself." So I hugged and kissed her and sent her off, silently praying, "O Lord, please let her know the way."

About a half hour later, there was a knock at the door. I opened it and a little girl rushed into my arms, sobbing as though her heart would break. It was Julia.

"Momma, oh Momma, I got lost. I can't find my school." Her face was wet with tears, and that started me crying too. I called Bob, and he came and took her to school. For the next two weeks, Irene, my next-door neighbor, walked with Julia until she could find her way to school alone.

With Mother happily occupied at the college and my girls both in school, I began to involve myself more in community life. I made many friends in church and on the block, gradually settling into a pleasant, unhurried routine.

Bob was working hard, long hours and often on weekends, but he never complained. However, he didn't seem very happy either, no longer talking about amusing incidents, often not talking at all.

One evening, when we had put both girls to bed, I decided it was time to talk it out. I asked Bob why he seemed so morose, so silent, "almost withdrawn lots of times." I could hear him take a deep breath.

"I guess I wasn't too good at keeping it from you," he said, ruefully. "I tried, but you always know when something is wrong, don't you?" Then he confided that he literally hated his job and had to force himself to go to work each morning. I pointed to the telephone.

"Get on that telephone and call the manager of that clothing store where you worked," I almost shouted. "You know he said you could always come back." Bob had worked in a large men's-wear shop and had made a good record. I was pretty sure they would take him back.

Well, it worked out as I had predicted. Bob was offered his old job, and once again, the Sanfords were on the move, this time returning to Coffeyville which we all considered our home no matter where we lived.

Shifting clouds. They floated away and the sun broke through again.

We moved to Coffeyville in August, just prior to the start of the school term, so that Stephie could enter second grade and Julia first, along with the other children.

Our house was in Edgewood, a new community west of town and across the street from the school, so there were no fears about the girls getting lost. It was owned by our very dear friends, Nancy and Robert Graham, who had just built a large house in another section of Edgewood. They agreed to rent us their old home and apply the payments to the purchase price if we decided to buy later on.

121

Our lives began to assume a permanence we had always wanted. I adored my new home. It was modern and well cared for, with all the conveniences that had been lacking in our earlier homes, despite their charm and our improvements. Bob was working very hard—he often came home for dinner and went right back to the store—but he liked his job and felt it had lots of opportunity for advancement.

As for the girls, they, too, had adjusted well to the move and were happy and healthy.

With house and husband and children active and happy, I began to get involved in the community once again. I rejoined our town's musical club, Matinee Musical, and was elected president.

Matinee Musical sponsored monthly programs and I was in charge of all the arrangements. I was very successful in getting volunteers to pitch in.

"How could I refuse, Charlotte?" one of my members asked. "Here-you are, blinded and doing all of this, as well as running a house and taking care of a family. Who could say they didn't have the time?"

Well, I tried not to make anyone feel guilty, but often I had a sneaking suspicion that I was asked to make these calls for that very reason. Anyway, I had no problem getting people to participate, bring cake, help in mailings, pick up fliers for Matinee Musical or for the PTA where I was also very active.

Bob and I went out a lot with Nancy and Bob Graham, and one evening we ended up at a neighbor's house where somebody started to play the piano and we all joined in. Bob's baritone rang out and I matched my tones to his—just as I had daydreamed in our dating days. Gradually the others became silent until only Bob and I were left singing.

I hesitated, but Nancy called out, "Don't stop, Charlotte. You and Bob sing so beautifully together." Well, that was the start. Bob and I began doing musical programs at parties, tailoring the songs to the occasion.

We sang in the church choir and also acted as sponsors for a student youth group. I began teaching a Sunday School class again and became the leader of a Brownie Scout troop.

Sigma Alpha Epsilon, a social sorority in Coffeyville, gave me its Diana award, presented annually to an "outstanding young woman in the community." That same month, I received a letter saying I had been selected to appear in the new edition of *Who's Who of American Women.*

But the clouds were gathering overhead again. Bob, as merchandise manager of the store, had the use of a car. One afternoon I heard his steps on the pavement outside the house. There had been no screech of tires, no sound of a car pulling to the curb.

I rushed to the door, calling out, "What's wrong?"

Bob's voice was very low as he answered, "I've been fired."

I took him in my arms and began to sob. "I'm sorry, I'm sorry," I said, over and over again. "What happened?" But Bob didn't want to talk about it. "Don't cry over me, please, Charlotte," he said quietly. And he went to the bedroom and closed the door. I knew Bob often wanted to be alone, to think things out, and I respected that. He began to look for another job but wasn't having much success when, once again, Jesus Christ showed His love through our friends.

Bob and Nancy came over for coffee one evening, and the four of us sat around the kitchen table chatting. We were talking about all sorts of inconsequential things, but Bob, my Bob, didn't have much to say.

Finally, Bob Graham also blurted out: "Bob, I hope this won't offend you; but Nancy and I have talked about your situation, and we have a suggestion. How do you feel about opening your own store?" He offered to lend us the money to get started.

The clouds began to drift away. Bob loved the retail

business, and he leaped at the chance to start his own. His voice took on an urgency I hadn't heard for a while. Coffeyville, he declared, had many women who were clothes conscious, who wore the latest styles and would welcome a chance to get them close to home.

He would open a ladies' boutique, stock it with the kinds of things available only in the big city—Kansas City —and customers would come flocking in. And that's how the Village Shoppe was born.

Bob found just the right location, signed the lease, and then went to New York and Dallas on a buying trip. His enthusiasm was contagious, and I felt at last we had come into our own—we had beautiful children, a lovely home, and now, a new business. We would have the place in the community we had wanted.

All of us—Bob, me, and the two girls—had parts in a production of *The Sound of Music,* which was being presented by the Coffeyville Community Theater. Bob was Captain Von Trapp, and the girls played two of the children, Louisa and Marta.

I didn't think there was anything I could do, but the children urged me to go down to the tryouts where I got the role of Sister Margarita, a nun. One of my friends, Joan Veron, was also a nun, and I clung to her arm while on stage. That way I could take part in what turned out to be a most successful production.

The show was presented in May, about three weeks before our shop was scheduled to open, so we put an insert in each program inviting the members of the audience to *our* premiere on May 24.

The night before the store opening, Mother and Nancy and Bob came down to help us arrange flowers, set up the displays, and mark prices on the merchandise. I walked around the racks, arranging the hangers and feeling the garments to make sure they were lined up straight. The tears streamed down my face, and I wiped them away before anyone could notice. And I thought, "Oh, if only Daddy were here to see and enjoy this!"

The Village Shoppe seemed to be exactly what Coffeyville ladies needed. There were lots of visitors—as well as buyers. Customers were charmed by the decor—early Colonial—and thought the clothes unique. Bob was happy and took to spending even longer hours in the store.

I didn't mind because I felt he was working for us, his family. I told myself that every new business demanded great dedication and just plain hard work.

But somehow, it seemed more than that. It seemed that a subtle change, hard to pin down, vaguely but persistently *there,* was coming over our marriage. I dismissed the thought when it first penetrated my mind, but it kept seeping back in.

It was a feeling spun out of fine threads. Just a little less talk between us. A little less time together. A little less warmth in the way he spoke. A little less love-making.

One evening, after a dinner during which he hardly spoke, though we were alone, the feeling intensified. The children had gone to Mother's house. When he rose from the table to return to the store, I put out my hand to stop him. I caught his arm.

"Bob," I said. "Is—is something wrong?"

"Wrong? What do you mean?"

I groped. "I don't know. I—well, I just feel left out these days. I don't seem to know much about what you're thinking or what's happening."

"For heaven's sake, Charlotte," he replied almost angrily. "You know how much I have on my mind. There's nothing wrong. But I can't just give you a play-by-play account of the day's events." He went out of the house.

But then I forgot about my qualms because I began feeling sickish in the mornings, symptoms not hard to recognize. I told Bob and said I thought I should see a doctor.

125

Julia's birth had been so difficult that my doctor had advised me not to have any more children. So Bob and I decided I should go to a specialist. We drove to Bartlesville, forty-five miles away. Bob was very quiet during the ride, the singing and running commentary he usually made on long drives absent. Most of the time, I silently prayed, for I wanted the baby more than anything else.

I continued praying as I lay on the table for the examination. When the doctor said, "Yes, Mrs. Sanford, you are pregnant," I was ecstatic. I could hardly wait to get home and share the news with the girls who had been asking for "a baby brother and sister" for a long time. We decided not to tell them, however, until the doctor completed the blood tests which would confirm his diagnosis.

I wanted to set the stage for our news as I had done when Stephanie was on the way. As soon as the doctor telephoned the results, I called Bob and asked him to come home for lunch. We were all sitting around the table when I said, "Girls, your father has something to tell you."

And Bob said, "Girls, your mother is going to have a baby." Well, they jumped up so fast they almost pulled the tablecloth and all the dishes to the floor. They screamed and hugged and kissed us. We were so excited—three of us, that is. Bob didn't play an active part in the gaiety and soon excused himself to go back to the store.

Shifting clouds, dark and ominous.

Bob was increasingly silent, but I decided it was worry about my health, not indifference. Those other hard deliveries must be preying on his mind, and after all, I was more than ten years older now.

Then the clouds collided and the storm broke.

On March 16, 1971, at 9:30 A.M., my world collapsed. The telephone rang and I picked it up.

I heard Bob's voice, but it sounded strange. I became

alarmed. "Is something wrong?" I asked quickly. A long silence and, as I started to speak again. Bob broke in.

"I tried to tell you a dozen times at home," he was saying, still in that oddly strangled tone, "but I couldn't. I just could not." He was rushing the words now. "Charlotte," he said, "I'm sorry I have to tell you this way, but you have to know that I don't love you any more."

And he hung up.

Chapter Eleven

I sat down. It was a long time before I realized I was still holding the telephone. I hung up and stared into my dark-gray world.

Time passed, but I remained in my inner and outer fog. I think I heard bells ringing. Maybe it was the phone or the door. I sat unmoving.

Stephie, then twelve, and Julie, who was eleven, came home for lunch and saw me slumped in the chair. I did not greet them with hugs, smiles, and a cheerful hello, as always, and they became instantly concerned.

"Mommy," Stephie asked. "What's the matter?" Almost literally, I shook myself. "It's nothing very much," I lied. Then, managing a little smile: "Just the new baby kicking up inside. I just felt a little sickish, that's all."

They ate their lunch quickly and skipped out to school. After they had gone, I went into the bedroom, stretched out on the bed, and wept, not understanding a bit what was happening, not understanding what happened to our love, what had gone wrong to shatter our lives.

In the afternoon, the girls returned from school and probably noticed my expression. They assumed, however, that I still didn't feel well and asked no questions. Bob came home, and we had dinner as usual. After homework and some TV-watching, I put the girls to bed.

Bob said little at dinner. When I removed the dishes and scraped the plates, I noticed he had barely touched his food. In the evening, after the children were asleep, I sat on the couch and, facing my husband, asked the single question:

"Why?"

It was all I said. I knew Bob; I was certain he was acutely aware that I deserved an explanation for the bombshell he had dropped upon me without warning. Though I was sightless, my ears told me what he was doing. I could hear that he swallowed hard. By the creak of an easy chair I knew he was shifting in his seat. A rustling of garments. He had crossed his legs.

"Charlotte," he said finally. "I don't know. I know that's hard to believe. Maybe impossible. But I don't know. It—it just happened."

I felt stings in back of my eyes. Tears were coming, and I bit my lip.

"Why did it happen?" I asked. "What *did* happen?"

"God, Charlotte," he said. "I wish I knew. I can't explain it to myself. How can I explain it to you? All I know is that—that—well, it's over."

He said he would try to make it as easy as possible for me. He would remain at home until after the baby came and would see to it that I was settled. Afterward, he would probably not remain in town, but wherever he went, he would make sure I received as much money for support as he could manage to send.

The store was not doing well, something I had known for some time. He tried everything he knew to reverse the downward trend, but nothing seemed to work. Perhaps he would sell it, salvage what he could. He just didn't know at that point.

He said no more.

Exhausted by the cataclysm that had torn apart my life so violently, I went to bed. I lay awake for hours, trying to sort out my thoughts, but my brain had turned to jelly and was unresponsive to my signals. My thoughts kept flying off by themselves, recalling bits and pieces of my past life like a movie trailer which offers snippets of a forthcoming feature. Bob and I meeting. Bob and I dating. The jukebox playing "Tenderly" the night I fell in love with him. Rising to my feet and screeching when he scored in a basketball game. Being pinned. That silly hunt for a ring that "looked like a bolt." The wedding, the children, the life together. I began to cry softly.

It would seem a brutal thing for a husband to tell his wife he no longer loved her only a few weeks before she was to give birth to his third child. I cannot soften the harsh truth. That was the way and that was the time it happened.

I am not being the least bit saintly about it. I believe in forgiveness, but I am frank enough to say that I was more deeply wounded by that shock than at any other time and by any other event in my life, and that includes my blindness.

And yet I know that Bob was not being intentionally cruel. It took a long time, but I came to understand that he told the simple truth when he said that he did not know why he said what he did, or why he chose to say it at that time.

If my emotions were torn apart by this horrendous, totally unexpected hammerblow, his had spilled over with an equal suddenness.

The next day was my birthday. The girls were in their usual frenzy; birthdays are always big things at our house. They darted around me like puppies, helping me set the table for a special dinner I always prepare. I heard the girls squealing as they bustled around, hanging up the "Happy Birthday" streamer, putting the special birthday napkins they had bought at the dime store at their places, decorating the dining room with rolls of crepe paper. Through it all, I forced myself to act cheerful and birthday girl-ish.

Then they shooed me out of the kitchen for their "surprise," the baking of a birthday cake. I was happy to leave. "I'll just rest in the living room," I told them. Their excited voices came to my ears as I sat on the couch. "They don't know," I said to myself. "Don't know that their world would be falling down soon too." They would be looking to me for strength. What strength did I have to give them?

Bob came home and, somehow, we got through dinner. It was a ghastly farce. Thankfully, the girls jabbered all through the meal and weren't aware that neither Bob nor I said much. After dinner, the girls marched in carrying their cake which, they told me, was decorated with "Happy Birthday Mother" and glowed with thirty-five candles. I stood, drew in a long breath, and blew. Then they—my family—sang "Happy Birthday" to me.

The farce still was not ended.

It was the night of our weekly choir practice, where it was customary to celebrate every member's birthday. There would be more cakes, one of which my mother had been baking and decorating for days; there would be gifts and singing and congratulations. And, because it was my birthday, my daughters would come with us.

I knew I looked dreadful. Could I plead illness because of my pregnancy? Exhaustion, some kind of virus? I couldn't disappoint the girls or my mother; I knew I had to go.

I got through that too. Managed to smile and accept the congratulations and listen to the "Happy Birthday" song again, exclaim over the little gifts. Bob handed me one, too. He had bought me a small radio with an earplug attachment I had always wanted. I didn't know how useful it would be for the sleepless nights that lay ahead of me.

Finally it ended, and I could go home to cry myself to sleep.

Mother had to be told. I shrank from that, but I couldn't put it off. Two days later, I blurted it all out to her.

"I don't know what happened or what I did," I said.

It seemed to me I had been repeating those same words a hundred times since the call came, but I couldn't think of anything else to say.

"The marriage is ended," I said. "Bob wants it that way."

Mother is a feisty person who has been through a great deal in life. She watched her daughter go blind, cared for a sick husband until he died, worked from the time she was twelve. She knew hardship and she knew tragedy. She didn't bewail her lot in years gone by and she wasn't about to start now.

"Charlotte," she· said in the same crisp tone she used when I wondered how I'd go through school, or care for my babies, or any other hurdle of my life. "Charlotte, you'll manage. You always have. You always will."

I listened and I wanted to believe her. My daughters were bright, capable, mature little girls for their age. But they were, after all, still preadolescent children. And, while Mother would help all she could, she had a full-time job as typist in a manufacturing plant and lived three-quarters of a mile away.

A few days after that shattering phone call, Joyce Logan, who had been away for a short time, dropped by the house. It was Tuesday, the day of our weekly Book Review Club where the newest books were discussed. Joyce and I had belonged for years.

Joyce was bright and chipper, as always. "Sorry to be late with it," she said as she thrust a large flat package into my hand. "But here's your birthday present." It was a record.

"What is it, Joyce?" I asked.

"The one you love so much."

I knew right away. It was a recording of the theme from the movie *Love Story*, which was so popular that year.

I thanked her, and we set out. On the way Joyce chattered about her trip and didn't notice my silence. I said nothing to her. At the book review session, Mrs. Marie Diggs talked about poetry. She read some selections from a recently published volume of love poems written by a Tulsa poet. I listened and began to weep softly.

Joyce nudged me. "Wow," she said, "you're sure romantic."

I had begun the period of self-examination all women go through when their marriages break up. Maybe (I was thinking) I hadn't paid enough attention to the outer manifestations of love. Maybe romance had seeped out of our marriage. Maybe wives should act more like lovers, give their husbands books of love poems like this, dress seductively, act like young girls on dates. Maybe I had become too drab, too much the mother, too much the housewife.

When the session ended, I stood out front unmoving. "Come on," Joyce said. "What's up? Still under the spell of those love poems?"

"I need to tell you something, Joyce."

She noticed the strange look on my face. "What's the matter?" she said quickly. "Anything wrong?"

All I could say for a moment was a whispered, "Yes." Then I regained control and told her the whole story, as fully as I knew it myself.

I heard a gasp of astonishment. "I can't believe what I'm hearing," Joyce said. "A perfect marriage like yours! You and Bob—I've never seen a couple who got on so . . . so well."

"I thought we did," I answered.

"You and Bob!" Joyce kept repeating. "It's unbelievable."

I was silent. It *was* unbelievable.

"Oh, God!" Joyce suddenly exclaimed. "And I just gave you that record. What rotten timing!"

We linked arms and walked home.

It was the longest month of my life. If we are loved, we can face anything. The greatest tragedy is not to be loved.

The night after Joyce gave me the record, the thought

133

of suicide crossed my mind for the first time. It was, I judged, about three in the morning, and I lay in bed sleepless. It would not be painful or difficult. Fill a tub with water. Step in. Lie down. Take the blade from a razor. Slash my wrists. Close my eyes. And die.

Why not? The thought penetrated a little deeper and grew more alluring in my mind. All agony would be blotted out in minutes, or however long it took. Why not? What was there to live for but a life of perpetual night, unloved and unwanted?

Suddenly I sat up in bed. Unloved? Unwanted? There were two children asleep in the next room and a third was even now turning in my belly. There was Mother, who had never wavered. And there was Jesus.

I banished the thought, and began to pray silently.

So Joyce knew and Mother knew, but nobody else. I thought I could keep the secret bottled up inside, telling nobody else. But it spilled over.

A day or two after my meeting with Joyce, Bob drove me to the home of the Reverend William Nelson and his wife Marge for a church committee meeting. Bill Nelson was pastor of our church, the United Presbyterian, and he and Marge had become dear friends, though we had known each other only a few years. Bill had arrived in town from McPherson, Kansas, about the same time Bob and I returned from Emporia. Marge, an accomplished musician, had accompanied Bob and me when we sang at church meetings—programs, I reflected, which often included songs of love.

I heard voices raised in discussion at the meeting, but I had no notion what was taking place. My body was there, but my mind was again flipping back and forth over my life with Bob, this time to the accompaniment of a buzzing sound in my head. I shook my head to clear it, but the buzzing remained.

Scraping of chairs told me the meeting had ended. Marge came over and said, "Stick around, Charlotte, Bill and I are going to take you home." I sat in a rocking chair, hands folded primly in my lap, until the other committee members had gone. Bill jangled his keys and announced he was ready.

Suddenly my mind cleared. The buzzing stopped. Still. seated, eyes straight ahead, I said in a low voice. "There's something I must tell you." I rested my right hand on the arm of the rocker and covered my eyes. The buzzing had started.

"I don't know what's happening to me," I continued. Marge and Bill had come closer and drawn up chairs. "What is it?" Bill asked, concern in his voice. "Is anything wrong?" I spoke slowly, my hand still covering my eyes.

"I don't know why this has happened, but—Bob doesn't want to be married to me any more."

The silence was total for more than two minutes.

Then Marge came to me and put her arms around me. "Are you sure? Are you *really* sure? Are you just imagining this?"

"No," I said, miserably. "I am certain. He told me, clearly and simply, in those very words." I turned my eyes toward her, and there were tears in them.

Bill came over and sat beside me. I know he could see the tension in my face and my swollen eyes. He helped me from the chair and into the car.

From that day, I spoke often to Bill who, with his wisdom, knew that I neither needed nor wanted pity.

One day he went to see Bob and, after a long talk, he came to the house.

"I have suggested that we don't do any counseling right now," Bill told me. "Bob will help make things as peaceful and as calm as possible these next weeks. Now listen carefully: You're not to discuss this any more with Bob. It will be hard, but discussing anything at this point will create tensions that could affect the baby. First things

135

first. We want you to take care of yourself and come out of this. We want a healthy mother and a healthy new baby."

So there was no attempt at counseling then, only the balm of prayer. I prayed alone, and we prayed together.

I cleaned house like a maniac, trying to keep busy. But there were just so many times I could vacuum the rugs and dust the furniture. I would lean on a broom and think hard. When did Bob's love begin to cool? My mind roamed over the past several years. There was the time he led me just a bit faster than usual as we walked to a meeting. I remember being a little out of breath—but I thought nothing of it because we were late, thanks to me as usual, and Bob probably wanted to make up the lost time. But there were other times, other incidents as the months went on. Yes, we *were* walking faster.

And he would forget to tell me about a step or a curb; I'd miss them, and my foot would slide off. And those times when he would help me into a car, he didn't open the door quite wide enough, and I'd scrape against the side just a bit. Or he would forget to tell me how much I had to duck my head, and a few times I'd bump it.

I did not think for a moment that Bob did any of these things intentionally. But were they signs that he was ceasing to care? That the endless task of acting as my eyes was becoming burdensome?

I recalled that, just a few months before, we had gone to a dance. I was feeling headachy, and the amplified rock music wasn't helping any, so I had asked Bob to take me home. "All right," he said, "if you want to go." His voice sounded tight. Riding home in the car, he was silent, and I realized he had wanted to stay. "Why don't you go back?" I said. "Look, I'll go to bed. I just can't take that blaring music." He said brusquely: "Forget it." We spoke little for the rest of the evening.

Our expressions of physical love had become less frequent, but I had not been especially concerned. I knew that when men are absorbed with their careers as their family grows, and the care of home and children drives women to exhaustion, sexual life can suffer. It was a fact of life, a cliché in TV situation comedies, even a joke among most married couples. But hadn't it diminished too much for us? I thought back and realized that our sex life had plummeted to near zero.

I remembered the night just after I had become pregnant for the third time. I drew close to him but felt him edge away. There was nothing wrong, the doctor had said, in making love during the early part of pregnancy; only in the last six weeks was intercourse expressly forbidden. But Bob didn't think we should, and we said goodnight. I lay awake, frustrated with desire, for hours. There had been other nights like that, before and after.

Too busy with the house and the children, I had not realized this was happening, but now I did. And wasn't there more? We had kissed often in the early years, as tenderly and as passionately as teenagers. But those kisses too had become fewer and more perfunctory.

Now the pieces fell into place.

Like my blindness, it had happened so slowly that I was not aware of its coming. Like people whose hearing is dimming, I could not detect the telltale signs. "There's none so blind as they who won't see," I said to myself and laughed, a little hysterically.

For there was no real mystery after all. Despite the poets and novelists who write of love everlasting and despite men and women who, like me, want to believe it, the blunt reality is that human love, like human life itself, can end.

Bob's stunning announcement to me that Thursday morning of 1971 was not calculated, nor was it the bolt from the blue it seemed. A volcano erupts suddenly and devastates a countryside with molten rock, but the superheated steam and gases have accumulated for a long time far below the surface. Suddenly one day the explosive forces break through

137

the plug of hardened lava inside the crater, and it all floods out. That was the way it happened with Bob.

But it wasn't until years after the agony had dulled that I would know this.

Meanwhile, I was left with a hundred questions and no answers.

The next weeks went by in a blur. I went about the business of living and being a housewife and mother. Bob and I spoke little, but I had much to do; and the children did not notice. We continued to go to Mother's for Sunday dinner, as usual; we went to church, and we sang in the choir.

On Sunday morning, April 18, a pain in my back woke me from a fitful sleep; soon it radiated on both sides to the front and became more severe. Labor pains had begun. I had wondered if, after eleven years, I would recognize them, but Mother had reassured me. "Don't worry," she had said crisply. "It's like riding a bicycle. You never forget." I didn't; on that Sunday morning, April 18, there was no mistaking them.

Mother, who had insisted on staying with us as my time approached, heard me in the bathroom. She scuttled in and asked if anything was happening.

I replied: "It's happening."

Returning to the bedroom, I woke Bob, who began to dress quickly, then went to rouse the children whom I wanted to come with us to the hospital in Bartlesville. In no time, they were dressed and announced they were ready. I turned toward them and grinned.

I couldn't see them, had not actually viewed Stephanie's face since she was three months and had not even seen Julie at all, yet I visualized them as clearly as though my eyes were perfect. They were standing there in the matching pink suits Mother had made for them, in stockings of lighter pink, their pink sweaters peeking out from beneath their jackets. And with big expectant grins on their faces. Julie wanted to know if they were going to watch the baby being born, but I wasn't that modern. "No," I told her, "but right afterward."

Bob emerged from the bathroom and asked me how quickly the pains were coming. "It's time," I said. "Then let's go," he said, and we trooped out in the early morning light to the car. Mother stayed behind to straighten up the house, planning to follow us in a few hours. Since Stephie and Julie had taken eighteen and twenty-one hours to come into the world, she figured there would be no special rush.

We drove west along Route 66 to meet 75, then turned south for the forty-five-mile drive. In the back seat, Stephie and Julia had taken out a big watch and were timing the pains. Bob, taking no chances, zipped down the highway. It was a two-lane affair, cracked and uneven, and I would scarcely recommend it as the ideal road for a woman about to give birth. Each time my uterus contracted, the hard ride intensified the pain; I bit my lips to keep from crying out.

We reached Bartlesville in twenty-five minutes. By the time we arrived at the hospital, just after 7:00 A.M., the pains were coming closer and closer together. In the lobby I kissed the girls and told them to remain in the waiting room as Bob announced my presence. I was rushed to the maternity ward, undressed, helped into a hospital gown, and put into the labor room.

A sheet was draped around my thighs, getting me ready for the internal examination. The pains were now rhythmic and frequent. I felt a hand in mine. Bob was there, standing by the side of the bed. I cannot remember what he said or if he said anything at all, but his very presence and the pressure of his hand was, at that moment, immensely reassuring.

I felt a sudden gush, and I knew that the "bag of

waters"—the amniotic sac inside the uterus which cushions the fetus as it develops—had ruptured. Nobody had to tell me what that meant. The baby would soon follow. I told the nurse, who asked Bob to leave. I felt her put a stethoscope to my bulging belly. She remained there for what seemed a long time, then I heard her footsteps as he left the room. The rapid click of her heels on the tile floor told me she was hurrying.

My ears picked up the sound of a clicking dial in an adjoining room. I heard the nurse's voice ask for the doctor. Her voice was low, and she had no idea, I'm sure, that my hearing was especially acute and that it would reach me. But it did and what she said turned me cold with fear.

"I can't hear the baby's heartbeat," she was telling him.

My lips moved in prayer. I was terrified that the emotional upset through which I had gone in the past month had injured my baby. The nurse returned just as a wrenching pain hit me.

She called for a stretcher, and I was wheeled into the delivery room. In less than five minutes, my son was born.

I held my breath.

The cry came, that wonderful cry of life beginning. His heartbeat had indeed been faint, and the doctor had been concerned. But it had not ceased, and he was alive.

God had given me a son.

They put him in my arms. In a few moments, the doctor stepped outside the delivery room and called to Bob, who was waiting nearby. The doctor gently took the baby. "Here you are, Mr. Sanford," the doctor told him, "here is your son." He handed Bob the tiny bundle, wrapped in a white blanket.

I will never know, nor would I ask, the emotions that must have surged through Bob as he held his son in his arms moments after birth.

In a little while, I was brought down to my room. Mother had driven up to the hospital at about nine, expecting to settle in for a long wait. She was greeted by two deliriously happy girls who lunged at her like linebackers, shouting in unison that they just got a baby brother.

The children were clamoring to see me and the baby. The doctor bent the strict rule against allowing children to visit patients and let them come up. The squealing of delight was so loud the nurse had to shush them. Stephie demanded the right to hold him on the way back home, saying it was only fair because she was older. Julie countered that that was no way to look at it because, after all, she was his sister too. I said we'd compromise: each would hold him half the way.

"What'll we call him?" Julia demanded. "What's his name going to be?"

I had already decided that. He would be Charles Robert, the Charles after my father, the Robert for my husband. But I would always call him Pete, the name everyone called Dad.

"Where did Grandpa's nickname come from?" Stephie demanded.

"Well," I said, "now don't laugh—but it came from a mule."

"A mule! Grandpa was named for a mule?"

"I guess you might say he was about the only person you ever heard of who was named for an animal instead of vice versa, but that's the truth. You see, your Great-grandma Akers had a very stubborn mule named Petey Barnum on her farm, and your grandpa was a very stubborn little boy, so one day, when he was very young, Grandma said in exasperation: 'I don't know who is more stubborn, you or Petey!' So from that day on, nobody called him anything else."

"Except me!" Mother said firmly.

"Anyway," I said, "he'll be Pete to us all, because Grandpa would have loved it."

The nurse brought Pete in and allowed the girls a

peek. They raised such bedlam that my three roommates were startled. Pete left with the nurse, and I hugged my daughters.

It was a joyous moment. I had forgotten Bob. He called to the girls that it was getting late and they had a long way to go. I knew he had been standing a little apart because he spoke from a corner of the room. His usually deep voice sounded muffled as though he was struggling to keep himself under control.

Chapter Twelve

I prepared to raise my family alone, beginning the first day home from the hospital.

Mother was waiting at the door, and I felt her reaching for the baby, but I refused to let her take him. I had set my goal. I would prove to everyone, especially myself, that I was capable of caring for him, the girls, and the house by myself.

I had made arrangements to have a maid come in and help Mother clean the place thoroughly—scrub the walls and floors, dust everything in sight and out, wash and starch the curtains. I wanted to start off on the right foot.

Unfortunately, I stubbed my toe right at the start. I placed Pete on the changing table, which I had asked Bob to set up in the bedroom in front of the window. All the things I needed were within reach, as they had been for Stephie and Julie more than ten years ago. I put one hand lightly on Pete and stretched out the other for a clean diaper. Then, with an audience of two little girls, a mother, and Bob, I felt for the pins, undid them, and removed the damp cloth.

I wasn't quick enough with the dry one. Pete released a stream which arched upward and drenched the newly-washed curtains. The girls howled. Never having cared for a little boy, I didn't know the fundamental rule that would prevent similar drenchings—namely, that little boys must never be left exposed. Off with the old, cover with the new, swiftly.

Well, I figured, it was only a little accident. The rest wouldn't be all that difficult.

Or would it?

Relatives and friends I had known all my life trooped into the house all that week, bringing presents, exclaiming over Pete, slapping Bob on the back, telling us how lucky we both were to have such a fine, lusty baby boy to balance off the family, how he was going to be a joy to both of us as we watched him grow, how fortunate we were to have not one but two "built-in baby-sitters"—our girls—and so many other things about familyhood and parenthood.

My self-confidence, which I had tried to build up in the hospital, soon evaporated as I realized that I was going through a charade, smiling my thanks, accepting their good wishes, agreeing with them that the future looked so bright. Few of them knew that, in a short while, this "happy home" they were describing would be breaking up.

It was, of course, the worst of times to try to deal with the dilemma. After childbirth, a woman's nervous system reacts more sensitively than at other periods in her life. Every mother knows that post-partum depression, the so-called "baby blues," is a very real phenomenon.

Sleep eluded me. When, after what seemed like hours, I did fall into a fitful slumber, I would have nightmares of wandering through dark crypts searching for a lighted exit, of my father staring at me with a look of infinite sadness, of violent thunderstorms interrupting the cherished family dinners we had on Grandpa and Grandma Akers's farm. I would come out of those dreams, like a swimmer emerging from deep water, thankful they were not real but terrified that, if I slept again, they would return. Wakefulness was better, even though it meant going through the days exhausted.

Bob wanted to leave and end the masquerade we were putting on for the town, but I needed more time. There were moments when I felt strong enough to do what had to be done, but the times of weakness, when my mind reeled with the enormity of the task ahead, were longer. I knew I wasn't ready. Looking back, I know that there was another reason for wanting to delay Bob's departure. Maybe—just maybe—a chance, however slender, remained to rekindle the love we once shared.

I was aware that I was humiliating myself, but I couldn't help it. I pleaded with Bob to stay awhile longer. He said he would, and we continued living together in our bizarre arrangement, the date for his departure undetermined, my future as blank to me as my view of the world.

One morning, while Pete was sleeping and the girls were at school, I lay on the bed and tried to nap. Suddenly I broke into a cold sweat and began to shiver. My heart began pounding with an unaccustomed rapidity and I felt myself growing dizzy and weak.

"I'm losing my mind," I thought in a panic. I rose, stumbled to the telephone, and called our family doctor. He was soon at the door.

He sat at the bed, took my pulse and blood pressure, and listened to my heart. Then he said in his low, kindly voice: "What's the matter, Charlotte?"

I lost control. "Help me, help me!" I pleaded. "I feel like the house was caving in on me. I think I'm going mad. Send me someplace!"

He took my hand. "What kind of place? Where do you want me to send you?" I blurted out the story. His voice sounded amused yet reassuring at the same time. "You know, Charlotte," he said, "women who have just had babies can have such vivid imaginations, and . . ."

Calmer now, I interrupted. "No, Doctor. It is not my imagination, and these are not the baby blues. He told me before I had the baby. It *is* true, and I do need help."

He assured me that the sweating, the heart-pounding, and all the rest were symptoms of an anxiety attack, but now he was convinced that my dilemma was real.

"Would you mind if I called Bob," he said, "and asked if he would want to see a marriage counselor or a psychiatrist?"

I turned my anguished face toward him. "I want to do anything that would help."

The doctor called Bill Nelson who came to see me. We talked a long while, and Bill, an alert and perceptive pastoral counselor, saw at once that Bob's continued presence in the house, far from reassuring me, was actually adding to my misery. By skillful questioning, he made me realize it too—that Bob's just *being* there kept reminding me of what I once had and soon would lose.

"Yes," I agreed, "I think Bob had better leave for a while."

"Do you want me to call him?" Bill asked gently. I nodded. "Maybe you should," I said, "because the more I talk to him, the lower I sink, the more I hurt, the more I am belittled."

Bill spoke to Bob that day and telephoned me. "Bob is going to move to a motel for a while," he said. I hung up and burst into tears. The end, wasn't it? The end, by easy stages?

Still, maybe not. Because Bob had agreed to go with me to see a psychiatrist in Tulsa. "Maybe," I told him, "he can help us see things we cannot see by ourselves." "Charlotte," he answered, "I'll go if you want me to." It was not reassuring, but we drove to Tulsa anyway.

On the way down, I could feel the thick wall of tension between us. At the psychiatrist's office, Bob was called in to see the doctor alone. Later, he described the session.

"You must feel a tremendous amount of hate for Charlotte," the psychiatrist told him, "or you would not be splitting up."

"No," Bob replied. "I don't feel any hate at all."

"But," the doctor said, "you should feel hate, or you would not be ending your marriage."

146

"Why should I feel hate?" Bob answered. "Nothing has happened to make me hate her, nothing at all."

Why, then, was he ending the marriage?

"Because," Bob told him, "at this point in my life, I don't feel a strong romantic emotional love for her."

My own session was not especially fruitful. Psychiatrists deal with the reality of life's events. And the blunt reality was that I must accept the fact that Bob was no longer in love with me. I didn't need a psychiatrist to tell me what I had known for months.

We drove back to Coffeyville.

Foremost in my thoughts was the realization that I had to tell the children that Bob would be leaving our home and that the marriage was breaking up. I dreaded it. I knew the strong bond that exists between fathers and their daughters. The girls doted on Bob and waited for him to come home each evening as impatiently as I had waited for my dad.

Would I be shattering their security, their sense of well-being with my words? I was certain they knew something was wrong—they could not have missed the chilly silences, the cutting words, the absence of happy camaraderie which occurred whenever Bob and I were together. Nothing had been said, however, and they had not asked. But I knew this could not continue.

There was a wedding at our church on Saturday night. Bill was performing the ceremony, and Marge was to play the organ. They picked me and the children up and took us to the church. Bob was to come for his clothes while we were gone so that the girls would not see him go.

I took the children into a small chapel where I had cried and prayed so many times in the past few weeks. I sat in a pew, holding Pete, with Stephanie on one side and Julia on the other.

"I have something to tell you," I whispered. I shut my eyes tightly to squeeze in the tears, but I could barely get the words out. I could feel Julia beginning to squirm beside me. Neither girl said anything.

"Daddy will not be home when we get back," I told my daughters. "He's moving out of our house."

Absolute silence, at first, then a storm. Both girls began to cry. "Won't we see him again?" Julia wailed. And Stephanie asked, almost pitifully, "Doesn't he love us any more?"

I kept a tight rein on my own emotions as I explained to the girls that their father and I had decided to live apart, that the love we had once shared no longer existed. I knew it was important that I not put Bob in a bad light, so I added that I was sure Bob would see them often and be available whenever they needed him.

In my halting explanation to the girls, I carefully avoided directing any bitterness or blame in Bob's direction.

The next day, I took the three children to church. Every other Sunday Bob and I would sing in the choir, but this time I sat in one of the pews, five-week-old Pete in my arms and the two girls beside me. Bob was not there.

My face burned. Now our friends and neighbors all knew that Bob and I had separated.

Bob and I had grown up in this little city. It watched me grow blind. It watched me get married, watched us be so much in love, do so many beautiful things together, have three lovely children. Now it was watching us break apart.

Mother and my close friends wanted to come over and help, but I wouldn't even let them inside the house. I had talked myself into a state of fierce independence.

I didn't reckon with bugs. Early in the week after Bob left, I walked into the bathroom and was literally dive-bombed by a dense swarm of them, coming at me from all sides. I beat a quick retreat and closed the door. I told the girls to use the second bathroom and next day called the exterminator. He explained that they were swarming ter-

148

mites that had been hiding all winter long and had emerged in spring to mate. "You had the light on, didn't you?" he asked. I told him the girls had just put it on. "That's the reason," he said. "They're attracted to the light."

Well, I learned more than I wanted to know about swarming termites, but at least I took care of them.

Days weren't so bad. There was so much to do and many calls from Mother and my friends, all wanting to know how I was doing. I was doing fine, I told them. But I wasn't, really. Because evening always came, the children always eventually went to bed, and then the loneliness would creep in. Those were the hours when my independence, so resolutely built up, began to crumble.

Night after night, I cried myself to sleep.

That Friday, Bob telephoned.

"Charlotte," he said. "Would you get my bathing suit and some things packed?"

"Oh," I asked. "Are you going to Kansas City to buy things for the store?"

"No," he replied. "I'm coming to get you. We're going someplace for the weekend."

If the roof had slid back and I'd seen a rainbow I couldn't have been more joyful. I felt sixteen again, the way I had felt when he called for our first date. I tried to keep my voice under control.

"What does this mean?" I asked.

"That we're going away for the weekend, you and I."

The mother in me: "But—what will we do about the children?"

"It's all arranged." He had called Mother, and she said she'd be happy to stay with the children.

I expected a miracle that weekend, but it didn't happen.

There was none of the fun and tenderness of the honeymoon days or the early years of our marriage. We walked around the grounds, saying little to each other. The spark

149

that had once ignited us was not there any more. Around us, I could hear the obvious enjoyment of the other couples, but we did not join in, though they were all pleasant enough to us.

We both knew the weekend would be a dismal failure, and we could hardly wait for it to be over.

Bob returned home with me, leaving the motel. He told me next day that he would leave the city as soon as he could.

Still, I wasn't giving up. I wanted him and was willing to fight to keep him and regain his love. No singer can hold a high C note continually, I reasoned. Love, too, can wane as a marriage goes through its stages. But just as it can dip, it can also grow in strength. Perhaps Bob could discover what ended his love for me. Perhaps he could be made to realize that what we had was worth keeping; and we both could be taught the steps to take to rebuild our once-loving relationship.

Counseling, I felt, could be the key. I urged him to come with me to Bill Nelson. He thought a long while, then agreed, though he asked that we go to another minister. I did not ask why but accepted at once. At the appointed time, we arrived at the rectory, and the minister invited us into his study.

I tuned into the office on the television screen in my mind. It smelled bookish and, I judged, was quite small because our voices sounded intimate, not lost as they are in more expansive rooms. The floor was tile, vinyl squares, probably. There was a desk, doubtless there for many years; when I brushed my hand against it, I felt the nicks and tiny scratches, wrinkles that come with age to furniture as they do to people. The minister's hand was cool, his voice low and pleasant. He led me to a comfortable chair and I sat, facing his voice. Bob was seated a yard away.

Someone once said: "Rich folks go to analysts with their problems, poorer ones seek out their pastors." There may be much truth in that because the vast majority of people in trouble find themselves seated in ministers' offices, as Bob and I did. That's no guess, either. Dr. O. Hobart Mowrer, who is a research professor in the department of psychology at the University of Illinois, has reported that the country's 350,000 clergymen "are undoubtedly seeing more people 'clinically' than all the psychiatrists, psychologists and psychoanalysts combined."

Cost is not the only reason. "The minister," writes Dr. R. Lofton Hudson, director of the Midwest Christian Counseling Center in Kansas City, "is a friend-at-large for the church and God. He goes to see people when they need him—in hospitals, in their homes and even in jails. Most ministers are 'on call' day or night seven days a week. It is assumed he has genuine concern for all people and especially for those in trouble. . . . No one else in our culture has precisely this role."

There is a built-in trust of the minister. For he is the man (and, increasingly now, the woman) who is committed to preserve the sanctity of marriage and the home. He marries us, baptizes our babies, helps us teach our children the meaning of faith, continually stresses in lectures and sermons the importance of family life. "Here," says Dr. Hudson, "is a man who has some ideas, at least, about how things go in a marriage. It is natural for people to turn to him with a marriage problem."

For these reasons, I felt a small surge of confidence as I walked into the study. But in a few moments, any hope I had was crushed because the whole naked, terrible truth became clear.

The full story of that session has been blotted out of my mind. I was talking about changing—what I could do to make things right between us again. Then Bob spoke and what he said was devastating. He hesitantly, quietly, let it finally emerge. He could no longer assume the burden

151

he had borne for the fourteen years of our marriage and, to a lesser extent, the years before that. He no longer felt able to be the eyes for a blind wife.

He had not wanted to wound me, yet he had thrown at me the one thing it was not in my power to change.

I shrank in my chair. I remember thinking that the weekend we both hoped would bring us closer only underscored the unbridgeable chasm that separated us. He had seen all the other couples playing tennis, volleyball, water-skiing, enjoying all the activities of seeing persons, and the contrast with his own life had been acute. Blind persons can certainly enjoy many forms of indoor and outdoor recreation; they can swim, bowl, do arts and crafts, square dance, social dance, sing, act. But none of the optimistic words about what blind people *can* do obscure what they cannot do. Bob wanted what I could not do.

There was little the minister could tell us after that. We left.

The next month was agony.

I still hung on to Bob desperately, trying to please him in every way I knew how, hoping he would stay. I bought a whole new set of lingerie. Maybe that would entice him and help. It didn't. I knew he hated to see me bite my fingernails. I stopped and made certain he saw them growing out. I even poured catsup on my steak, something I abominated, because I knew he did it.

On Julia's eleventh birthday, my control broke and, for the first time, I became hysterical—and before the children. We had planned a swimming party. Mother was in the kitchen getting the cake, ice cream, and everything ready. I went down to help her and suddenly the dam broke. I leaned against the wall and began to sob, great, heaving, body-racking sobs. Everything that had been locked inside me came out, and there was no way to stop it.

I slid to the floor and, my back against the wall, repeated over and over, "Why? Why? Why?" Both girls had heard and ran down. They were crying too, and I couldn't stop.

After ten minutes, I finally regained control, and we went on with the birthday party. I am sure it was one of the saddest parties Julia ever had.

Looking back, I know I should have let him go sooner because the longer I held on, the more he resented being held. One night he lashed out at me. I won't ever forget the words:

"Charlotte," he said, "you're always going to be a burden to your mother, to your children, and to your friends."

I know now that, while the words came from his lips, it wasn't Bob at all who was talking. Perhaps he was hurting me so that I would stop my absurd attempts to cling to something I should have known was dead beyond revival. Perhaps he spoke out of fear, anger, and frustration. The fact that the store was doing so badly was no help either to his peace of mind.

But I was unable to reason then. I just heard the words, and they burned into my mind.

Late that night, after Bob was asleep, I slipped out of bed and went silently into the bathroom. Before Pete was born, I had had the strength to dismiss the thought that had come to me. Now it came again, more forcefully, more irresistibly than before. I was going to end my life.

For the first time in months, I felt strangely calm. My mind seemed to work clearly. Everything had to be done cleanly, efficiently. I have always been a meticulous person, and I must not make a mess out of the final act. I would cut my wrists in the bathtub and let the water run so that it would wash the blood down the drain. All they would find in the morning would be a lifeless body. I had it thought out to the end. The children would not see me first; Bob, who always rose first in the morning, would make the discovery and then tell them.

Why should I stay alive? My husband had told me that I was a burden to my mother and my children, to him and to my friends, and I believed him. Bewildered by the incredible turn events had taken, I was making mistake after mistake at home, burning the roasts, forgetting the vegetables, tripping over things I always was able to maneuver around before. I would never be able to help my children with their school work, never be able to be the kind of wife Bob wanted. Why should I stay alive?

I locked the bathroom door, opened the medicine chest, and felt for a razor. I opened it, removed the blade, and placed it on the rim of the bathtub. I ran the water, waited several minutes, then slipped out of my night clothes and stepped in.

I felt for the blade and held it carefully between my thumb and forefinger.

I was being logical, sensible. Why not? If there are Four Horsemen of the Apocalypse there are the three basic impelling causes of suicide. The first is loneliness, and I felt enveloped by it. The second is helplessness to change matters, and I was powerless to change the thing that was causing my hurt. The third is hopelessness, and I was assailed by feelings of futility. I felt trapped by the circumstances of my life. I was on the roof of a burning building with no way to escape.

The blade was touching my wrist when I stopped it. I could not explain then, nor can I now, what happened. There was no signal, no word, no sign, no thought, no special glow that entered my mind and spirit. I know it would sound a great deal more dramatic if I could say that I received a sudden flash of insight, a signal. I did not.

All I am able to say is that somewhere in the depths of that private hell, in the pit of darkness into which I had fallen, Jesus Christ found me and gave me an infusion of courage to bear what had to be borne. It is as simple—or, perhaps, as profound—as that.

I believe that Jesus lifted me out of hell that night. He did not allow me to take my life. He gave me what I needed most—the single, priceless ingredient that gave me the strength to face life—the feeling that I had *worth* as a human being.

We are all children of God, and not one of us is worthless, no matter how inadequate we may feel to cope with problems of day-to-day living.

My mind now clicked fast, like snapping the controls of a slide projector. Okay, I was worthwhile. From there, it is only one tiny step to hope, for being worthy means being *important*. Next slide. If I am important, how then can I be a total, hopeless burden to my family and the world? My entire life had been a succession of large problems and small ones, just as everyone else's has been and always will be. I had done pretty well with mine, hadn't I? Knowing this added to my now-growing conviction that the strong likelihood was that I could solve this great one too, adequately enough.

Yes, for the moment, I was trapped on the roof of a burning building. But I realized now that I did not have to jump. I had a fire escape—the love of God. And nobody who has the love of God is without hope.

Oh, I knew there would be no instant solution. There would be times of confusion and doubt, of acute anxiety about the future, and many tangled thoughts and feelings.

But I also knew in that moment of time that I did not have to resort to what Dr. Karl Menninger, the eminent psychiatrist, has called the "malignancy of self-destruction" to find peace. I could find my own peace, using my own strength.

That was my great discovery that night.

I rose from the tub, replaced the blade in the razor, put it back in the medicine chest, and shut the door. I dried myself and returned to my bedroom.

155

Chapter Thirteen

On July 31, fourteen years after it had begun, my married life ended. Bob drove away. As the sound of the tires receded in the distance, shaken and confused, I sank to the floor.

"God," I cried out, "you've been with me every bit of the way. You know I will try. But I'm scared. I've got three little children, very little money, and lots of debts. Can I do it?"

The next morning, August 1, a friend drove me to the Coffeyville Bank where I signed papers transferring sole ownership of the Village Shoppe to me. My assets now consisted of an almost bankrupt ladies' boutique, about $100,-000 in the red, a bank balance of $1,000, and a heavily mortgaged house.

Jack Lively, my lawyer, sat me down in his office and tried to explain my financial setup.

"You won't be able to draw any money from the business," he pointed out, "because it's on the verge of bankruptcy. Maybe we'd better see if you can get any help from the welfare agencies."

"Jack," I cried, "I can't. I can't accept welfare. No matter what, I don't want to ask for charity." Jack told me I had no choice. Later, when Bob got a job and began earning money, there would be a separate maintenance agreement stipulating how much he would contribute. Bob couldn't give any money for support now, and the children and I had to eat. It was as simple as that. I rose from the chair and went with him to the welfare office in downtown Coffeyville. I had always wanted to be a social worker, had majored in sociology in college; and now I was to be on the other side of the fence. I was devastated.

Jack led me to an office and guided me to a chair. I heard a rustling. A paper was being pushed across the desk toward me, I surmised. I heard Jack tell someone: "She cannot see," and a woman's muffled, "Oh." Then the woman began to ask questions about me and the family. I heard the sound of writing as she put my answers on a form.

"How many children do you have?" she asked. "What does your husband do for a living?" I whispered my responses. I know she could barely make them out, but I couldn't speak any louder. I felt completely humiliated.

"Do you have any source of income?" was her next question. "What do you estimate your expenses to be?" She was pleasant enough, but the whole experience was shattering. I started to get up to leave, but Jack pushed me down.

Finally, the woman told me to "print your name and address and sign on the bottom line." Very matter-of-factly, she said, "You'll hear from us." We were finished, and Jack led me to his car.

It was about a month before the first relief check came, alloting us $198 a month plus food stamps and medical and drug expenses. I sent Stephanie to the store for milk and eggs. She came back about half an hour later, clutching the bundles. Years later she told me how embarrassed she was when she had to buy something with food stamps.

The morning after the visit to the welfare office, I awakened early and left home to begin a totally new part of my life. I knew nothing of the business world, had never seen an invoice and barely knew what it was. Bob did not want me to work, and I was content to be a housewife and mother.

Now, however, I knew I had to be more. There were two people already employed in the store—an elementary school teacher named Charlotte Argent who would return to her class in the fall, and Jackie Cambron, a part-time high school clerk. I had to learn how to run a business fast.

Maurice Weinberg, who owned a store in town, called me and said, "Charlotte, I want you to know that any time I can help you, anything you want to know, just call me." Poor, sweet man, I've often wondered if he was sorry he offered because I must have called him at least ten times a day for the next three months.

Because the store was in such poor financial straits, Bob and Nancy Graham, who had supplied the money to get us started, suggested a liquidation sale.

"That will accomplish two things, Charlotte," Bob Graham pointed out. "It will help you move some merchandise which has been around awhile and also supply some ready cash. You can use that to put in a new line and get started again."

It made sense so we started planning. Nancy called Bob, my Bob, and enlisted his aid.

"You're a fine artist," she told him, "and you know the inventory. Charlotte doesn't. You'll have to help out."

Bob came down and worked all that night. He made a huge sign advertising the sale for the front window. Then he went through the entire stock, marking the prices down and making smaller sale signs for inside the store. The next day, crowds started forming before the doors were open.

I'm afraid I wasn't too helpful when the sale started. I'd never sold a dress in my life. But I listened carefully to everything that was said. It is remarkable how much information I was able to absorb from the bedlam. If I was now to be a storekeeper, I would be the best. I would learn everything I needed to know.

Helped by Maurice Weinberg and Mrs. Argent, I learned about store and inventory control, pricing, invoices, profit margins, taxes, insurance, and record-keeping. Previously, Bob had done all the buying. Now it was up to me. Mrs. Argent had gone on these trips with Bob and she volunteered to be my guide.

On the way to the buyers' market in Kansas City, she explained the whole procedure. "Each company has a booth," she told me. "The salesmen display the merchandise and the buyers make their selection." She told me these markets were held several times a year, before each selling season, and this was how Bob had stocked the store.

"How on earth can I select clothes when I can't see them?" I wondered aloud. "It's not just for myself now. If I make a mistake, we can lose thousands of dollars."

She assured me everyone would help. She was right. The salesmen knew Bob; but when it was explained that I was running the business now and I could not see, they laid out the skirts, the blouses, and the jackets on a table where I would run my hands over the material and finger the garments to pick out details of the style. The salesmen described the colors. I was deluged with advice about which articles went together.

I had a little trouble reconciling some of the suggestions about color and objected vigorously when one of the salesmen described the virtues of matching a green blouse and a blue suit. "I know what colors are," I told him sharply. "I was once able to see greens and blues. They don't go together."

I gave in meekly when it was explained that manufacturers now used many different hues of colors and, yes, indeed, blue and green was now a popular combination.

I learned to make decisions quickly. Market was a fast-moving thing and you didn't loiter at the booths. You "looked" at the goods, bought, and moved on to the next stall. I soon felt my way about the clothes very quickly, and I was able to develop mental images of styles and colors and prints by listening carefully to sales descriptions.

We had to do a lot of buying in one day because the store could not stand the expense of a two- or three-day out-of-town trip. It was an exhausting experience, but I became so adept at it that I was able to calculate my expenditures as I went along so that I would not go over the budget in any one area.

Sometimes salesmen would come to the store, put their wares on racks, and roll them inside. I liked this better because it wasn't as frantic as going to the market. I could take a little more time to get the feel of each garment and make my decisions. I did very little actual selling. I spent most of my time in the back room where I had my office.

Going over the stock and deciding what to buy was one of the things I liked to do best. How could a blind lady do this? My assistant would go through the inventory first. Then she would come to me, saying, "Charlotte, it's time to order again. Let's get going."

We would go to the racks, and I would run my hands over each garment. She would tell me how many we had stocked originally and how many were left. "This one seemed to walk out the store, Charlotte. We sold every piece except this one. We need something like that next season."

And so we would go through all the merchandise, and I would either order or drop some lines. It was also my responsibility to answer telephone queries and dictate responses. Customers were sometimes astounded when I would check the fit of a garment after it had been pinned up for alteration. By feel, I could tell if the shoulders fit properly and if the collar was flat. By using the customer's knee as a guide, I could easily tell her if the hem was the right length.

Mother was the bookkeeper; and after working for eight hours at her job, she would come by late in the afternoon to balance out the books and take the money to the bank. We'd have supper together, and she'd play with the kids and go home. She was working terribly hard, but she never skipped a day. I could not have managed without her.

Toward the end of the summer, Mrs. Argent reminded me that she would be returning to school soon and that I would have to start looking for someone else to help me. Although I had learned a great deal about business management, I could not be alone in the store.

People have said, "Everything that's happened to you is a coincidence." I don't believe that. I know that nothing that happens in life is coincidence. It's the work of God. Bad things have happened in my life, but God does not make things happen to you. However, He can help you work out your trials and your tragedies into something beautiful if you'll only let Him.

How else can I explain that before I could advertise for an assistant, I got a telephone call from Lucille Dunbar. She was a devout Christian woman, recently divorced, who had heard somehow that I would need a replacement for Mrs. Argent.

"I would like to come to visit you, Charlotte," she told me. "I think I can help." Lucille wanted to work for me. She had no experience in a store; but she loved clothes, was very organized, and was sure she could learn the ropes quickly. She proved to be right.

She was really a messenger from God to help me in the store and in my emotional life as well. We prayed together; we worked together; we laughed together. She had been through a divorce and knew the meaning of hurt. She knew how to cope with it, and when she could sense from my mood how I hurt, she could provide comfort.

Slowly the store began to make money, and I started to pay off bills. The original backers, Nancy and Bob Graham, decided to reinvest their funds. I still owed them more than $70,000, but they said they were willing to lend me more because they had faith in Jesus Christ and they had faith in me.

"If anybody can do it, you can," Bob said. I know they hoped to get some return on their money, but equally important to them, they knew the store kept me mentally and emotionally, as well as physically, busy.

Busy as I was, I worried a great deal about the children. I felt especially guilty about Pete who was only three months old, and it broke my heart to leave him to go to work. I had always been home with my girls and given them lots of tender loving care. I felt I was cheating Pete because I wasn't able to expend the same amount of time and energy for him. During vacation, the girls pitched in, but I dreaded the start of school.

One day at work, the telephone rang. It was Sally Holliday, a member of my sorority, who said, "Charlotte, Ralph and I would like to take care of Pete. We'll pick him up in the morning, take him home with us, and return him home when you are there."

Sally had been to a sorority meeting the night before. I wasn't going out yet, but Mother, who was one of the sponsors, did. The girls plied her with questions. "Is there anything we can do?" one of them asked. "Just remember her in your prayers and call her if you hear of a good baby-sitter," Mother responded.

That was behind Sally's offer, and as I listened to her words, I thought, once again, Jesus had guided someone beautiful into my life. "I can't believe this," I told Sally. "This is an answer to my prayers."

"Will you let us do it?" Sally quietly asked. And I said, "Yes. Thank you."

Sally and Ralph, her husband, are special people. They are both extremely intelligent, college graduates and wonderful, devout Christians. They live on a huge farm where they looked after Pete for five years before school and every summer since he entered.

Pete calls Sally, "Nanny," and Ralph, "Boss," and loves them as his "second parents." Sally helped Pete explore the beautiful, simple things of nature. Ralph took him all over the farm, gave him routine tasks as he grew, and taught him the value of work. I think Pete was reading at three because Sally took the time to sit down and teach him.

That first morning, as I heard Sally drive away in her Scout, a heavy-duty farm car, Pete and his pillow strapped down beside her, his diapers on the seat beside him, I thanked God again for Sally and Ralph Holliday.

Arrangements had to be made for the girls as well. I couldn't be home at noon, so Julia was invited to have lunch every day with her friend Kathy, who lived on the same block. Steph went to school in town, so Mother would pick her up, and they would have lunch together in Mother's apartment. Thus, all three children were cared for, and I could devote myself to the store during the day.

It was in the evening, at home, that the depression would return. I was trying to do all of the tasks I had done before—except I was now doing them after 5:00 P.M. I forced myself to clean the house, spend time with the children, fix the meals, all after putting in eight hours in the store.

I got only three or four hours sleep a night. Once I mopped the kitchen floor at three o'clock in the morning. Tears began to stream down my face, and I suddenly began to sing "Living for Jesus," the hymn I had heard when I was eight and I decided to give my life to Christ. Once again I was singing it, only this time in the middle of a crisis I could not have anticipated.

After supper, the girls would clear the table and wash the dishes while I took care of Pete. As I scrubbed his chubby legs, I cried. Sometimes I didn't even make it that far. I'd come through the door and just collapse, sobbing, in a chair. Julia would immediately take over with Pete, and Stephanie would take me in her arms and try to comfort me.

Stephanie was only twelve years old then and Julia

was eleven, but life was making greater demands on them than is usual. They were marvelous all through those dreadful times and developed a maturity and wisdom far beyond their years.

Bob and I kept in touch because I still had so many questions about the business. One night, after we talked on the telephone, I dropped the receiver and began to cry.

Stephanie heard me in the next room. "Julia," she cried out, "watch Pete. I'll take care of Mother." She cuddled me in her arms until my sobs quieted—a twelve-year-old girl caring for a thirty-five-year-old mother who was falling apart.

Stephanie was strong then, but she began having problems when she entered the junior high. She would faint in school. Once she fell down a flight of stairs because she lost consciousness as she was about to descend. Fortunately, she did not hurt herself, but I took her to the doctor for a checkup. He found nothing physically wrong and suggested I consult a psychiatrist.

We went to see my former psychiatrist. I hadn't been there for a couple of years, and he remarked on how well I looked. I confided my fears about Stephanie.

"Charlotte," the psychiatrist explained, "a divorce doesn't only involve a husband and wife. Children are deeply affected, even when the circumstances are friendly. They miss the other parent and long to be like their friends, most of whom have both a father and a mother.

"Your daughter hid these feelings at the time of the divorce. She may be unaware even now of being lonesome for Bob." He diagnosed Stephanie's illness as a form of hysteria and suggested we see a child psychiatrist. We took his advice, and Stephanie has worked out her problems and grown to be a beautiful, mature young woman.

Julia was always the one who took care of Pete. Julia, a "mother" since she was one year old, was constantly dressing, changing, and feeding her collection of dolls.

When Pete came along and I fell apart, she took over with a real child.

I felt very secure when my eleven-year-old daughter cared for my son. I could hear her talking when she fed him.

"Come on, Pete, you've got to eat this. You've got to grow to be a big boy."

Chapter Fourteen

The days passed and suddenly it was Christmas, the first one without Bob. I wanted it to be as gay and happy for the children as it had always been. As for me, I was more lonely than ever at what used to be the most special time of year. But I kept the loneliness and the memories locked inside.

It was Pete's first Christmas, so we went all out. Mother came over and cooked and baked, and soon the house was full of gorgeous holiday smells. Stephanie and Julia went out shopping for the tree. We strung popcorn, bought tinsel, and brought down the old, familiar ornaments from the attic. Each year, when we had taken down our tree, we had carefully packed them away. Now, Mother and the girls undid the wrappings and exclaimed anew over each colored ball and twinkling light. Julia tried to explain to Pete why all this was happening, but I'm afraid it was hard for an eight-month-old to comprehend.

On Christmas Day, my aunt and cousin had dinner with us just as they had in years past. It was a difficult day for me, and I was relieved when it ended. The next day was Sunday, and Bob came to pick up the children. As they left, with Bob carrying Pete and the girls chattering about their Christmas presents, I could feel the depression beginning to set in.

Quickly I left the house and went to church where we worshipped the Lord and then had a breakfast to celebrate His birthday. My spirits rose, but when I went home the inner darkness took over again. I knew my minister and his wife had left that afternoon for a vacation, but I needed help, so I called the minister of another church in town. He could tell I needed counseling immediately. A friend drove me to his home.

I told him about another blind person who had ended her life not long before. "You know," I said, "maybe she knew something I didn't know. Maybe she was wiser than I am. Maybe all those things Bob said were true. Maybe she was right, and there is only one way out of this."

I was horrified by what I heard myself saying. Many months before, I had been convinced that thoughts of ending my life would never again recur, yet once again they were seeping into my mind. We talked for a long time that afternoon, and when I left I felt again that God knew I had worth, that Jesus loved me and that I had to go on for the children's sake, if nothing else.

Slowly I reentered the social life of the community. Nancy and Bob came for me, and I went, for the first time, to a small party attended by many of the couples my husband and I had known. There were other parties, each easier for me than the one before.

The store showed a profit in our second year. Bob got a job and began to send money, so finally we were able to go off welfare. Lucille, my assistant, decided to move away from Coffeyville, and I had to replace her. Fortunately, someone I knew wanted the job.

Just after I had hired Lucille, a neighbor of mine, Betty Swanson, called and asked about the job. "I've already promised it to someone, Betty," I told her, "but I'll certainly remember you if I need help again." I immediately thought of her when Lucille gave me notice. Betty talked it over with Roy, her husband, and the next morning the telephone rang before I left for work.

167

"I'd really love to, Charlotte," she declared. "You know how crazy I've always been about clothes. I think it will be lots of fun, and I'm sure I will be able to help you."

It turned out to be a splendid arrangement. Betty was just what I needed in my life at that time. She was about ten years older, outgoing, and knew a lot about styles.

As a matter of fact, not only did I get Betty, I got Roy as well. He was always in and out of the store and handled many chores that would have been difficult for women. Roy lifted boxes, helped create window displays, and put up the outdoor Christmas lights one year. In addition, they both became my very good friends.

I juggled chores at home and store, careful always to spend as much time as I could spare with the children. In the spring of 1972 I began to think positively about acquiring a leader dog.

Leader or guide dogs were trained by the Germans after World War I for returning soldiers who had been blinded in battle. Today they are used extensively by sightless people in everyday life. The dogs take their masters through city streets, avoiding possible hazards and weaving their way even through heavy traffic. More than ninety percent of the guide dogs are German shepherds, although Labrador retrievers, boxers, and Doberman pinschers are equally adaptable for the job.

There are about a dozen centers for training guide dogs in the United States, the best known being The Seeing Eye, Inc., founded in Morristown, New Jersey, in 1929. Not everyone is given a guide dog—applicants must undergo a stiff screening before being accepted, then spend some four weeks in a tough, concentrated program which teaches the care and use of a dog. More than ninety percent of Seeing Eye graduates are holding down jobs or are otherwise usefully occupied. Lions International, the great organization of business and professional men founded in 1914, has a school in Rochester, Michigan, where blinded people are trained to use "leader dogs."

I called my minister, who was a member of the local Lions Club and told him I wanted a dog. The Lions handled all the arrangements, supplied me with an airplane ticket, and, two weeks later at the beginning of June, my family accompanied me to Tulsa where I set off, alone, on my first plane ride.

I was somewhat apprehensive about traveling alone, but as I felt the plane take off smoothly and begin to rise in the air, my spirits perked up considerably. Still, I wondered just how I was going to manage my first meal alone.

As luck—or God—would have it, the man sitting next to me began to speak. "I have an aunt who is blind," he told me, and we began to converse while all about us, the flight attendants prepared to serve lunch. When the tray was placed before me, my companion, quietly and without being asked, described the food and the location of each utensil.

The remainder of the trip was without incident, and we soon landed in Rochester where I was met by one of the instructors who led me to the bus where other members of my training class had assembled from all over the country.

Four of us were assigned to a room and immediately set about unpacking and confiding information about ourselves and the little we knew about the rigorous program which awaited us. As I listened to the chatter from girls I judged to be much younger, feelings of homesickness began to overwhelm me. I missed my children terribly.

The next day, the training began with an orientation program at which the school's regulations were explained. We would not be allowed to leave the grounds and could not receive any visitors, even family. It sounded to me like I was in prison, but I soon understood the very good reasons. We were going to be taught to fend for ourselves, with the aid of our dog, and without the help of well-meaning friends or relatives. And, until we could do that, we could leave the grounds only with an instructor.

Gwen, a black girl from Mississippi who was one of

my roommates, was in my group. A strong, friendly man who was our trainer and leader began to work with us that same day. "Here, Charlotte," he directed, "grab this." He thrust what seemed to be leather straps into my hand. I felt it carefully.

"It's a harness," I said. I felt some more. "And there's a circle at the end." The trainer explained that such a harness would be worn by the leader dog. The "circle" was a metal hoop covered with leather which we would hold when walking with our dogs.

For the next few days the trainer acted as the leader dog. He would hold the harness and we would walk with him, fingers lightly grasping the hoop.

"The dog is trained to walk at a normal pace," he told us. "He will stop at curbs so that you know when you will have to step down. He will watch the traffic so that he can take you across safely. Trust him."

With the trainer as the "dog," we left the school grounds, went up and down curbs, crossed streets, practiced the commands for "right," "left," "forward," and "halt." Finally the trainer decided we were ready to receive our dogs. He said the dogs had been matched to their masters on the basis of size, age, temperament, and personality.

"Your dog is named Polly, Charlotte. She's a black Labrador retriever." I swallowed hard. I had never been an animal lover, but when I decided on a leader dog I was hoping for a golden retriever. Many years before, a neighbor had one, and I had admired their long silky hair.

However, I stopped thinking about that and listened again to my trainer. "When I come to the door," he explained, "I'll tell you I'm here and you call her name."

I was the last in my room to get my dog. I could hear the other girls, hugging their dogs, talking to them, and wrestling with them. Was I going to be able to do that?

Finally, I heard the trainer call out: "Charlotte, I'm here." I said, "Polly, come here." A dog bounded over to me and licked my face and hands and, before I knew it, I was down on the floor, too, petting my dog and getting acquainted. Later I called home and told the children about Polly. They dragged out the encyclopedia and read to me every word about Labrador retrievers. They wanted me to bring the dog home immediately, but I had to learn to follow Polly, to work with her and have confidence that I could trust in her.

Two and a half weeks later, Polly and I were in an airplane, bound for Kansas City and home. Sally and Ralph Holliday and Jack Lively had brought Stephanie and Julie to meet us at the airport, and we had a tearful reunion. Sally told me later how "marvelous it was to see you walking across the landing field, with Polly leading."

Polly was restless on the four-hour drive home, and I had to pet and reassure her. I needed plenty of reassurance myself—I was certain that Pete, who was only about eighteen months old, would have forgotten me.

When he saw me and called, "Mama," I burst into tears.

Polly accompanied me everywhere. We went on long walks on weekends, just around the streets or to the grocery if I ran out of something at the last minute. I would be driven to work, with Polly sitting in the back seat of the car and, when we arrived, she would jump out of the car and wait while I grabbed hold of the harness. She would lead me into the store and wait until it was time to leave. I began to realize that when I had Polly, I could be independent and did not always have to have another person around to take me places.

While I was away at Leader Dog School, Mother and Betty ran the business—with the aid of the long-distance telephone. Calls went back and forth between Coffeyville and Rochester as we conferred on what to buy for the coming fall season. Sales were up, and the financial statements were healthy.

In the summer of 1972, Marilyn Lively, Jack's wife, and Glenna Harrell, who was a new member of my prayer group, tried to persuade me to join them for a week's stay at a Christian camp in Missouri.

I wasn't too enthusiastic at first. "It's going to cost more than I can afford," I told Marilyn, "and, anyway, I can't leave the children for such a long time." But Marilyn would have none of this.

"Listen, Charlotte," she insisted, "Jack and I want you to go. We'll pay for it, and you can take the girls as well." She had already spoken to Mother about baby-sitting with Pete at night, and Mother was on her side. So all my objections were taken care of, and I had no choice but to go.

It turned out to be a beautiful experience. The main speaker was Reverend Cliff Custer, who talked of Jesus with such great love and wisdom that he made Him even more real to me than He had been before.

The week's program included large prayer meetings, smaller group sessions, and individual counseling with Reverend Custer. I had several counseling sessions with him and told him I was still trying to get over the loss of Bob. He prayed with me, and for me. I asked him to pray for Bob, "because he needs you too." While I was attending these sessions, Stephanie and Julia went to special meetings arranged for the children.

Probably that one week of concentrated prayer and counseling, of teaching and learning, helped me more than any psychiatrist could have done in several years. I came home a different person, an even deeper Christian, with new ideas and a new joy and excitement in my faith.

In the next few years, I went many times to meetings run by evangelical ministers in Coffeyville. I recall vividly a three-day meeting held by John and Paula Sanford, again no relation of Bob's. John spoke quietly, no rip-roaring, screaming, and stomping for him—or for me. I never went to meetings where people yelled and carried on. I'm a quiet person, so I always chose quiet people to listen to.

"Is there anyone here who has anything they think they need to be forgiven for?" he asked. Slowly I raised my hand. I heard a voice behind me say, "Boy, those Presbyterians sure are sinners." I almost laughed aloud. I learned later there were two other hands raised, those of my daughter and a close friend. The speaker was right. All the sinners that night were Presbyterians.

Paula and I went into another room, and I confessed to a sin I had committed many years earlier—a sin which I knew the Lord had forgiven, but I was not able to. I'm not going to discuss it now, though people have since told me it "was not so bad"; but at that time, I felt it was blocking the close relationship I wanted with Jesus Christ.

Paula and I talked. I can still feel the anguish and heartbreak of those moments. She prayed for me, and then we prayed together. Gradually I came to understand why I had committed this sin, and everything fell into place. I had been forgiven by the Lord, and I could now forgive myself. I no longer had any guilt.

The next night, at the meeting, John asked, "Are there any of those who would receive the baptism of the Holy Spirit?"

I whispered to myself, "Lord, I want the baptism of the Holy Spirit, but I don't want to be embarrassed because you know how I am." I fought my timidity and again raised my hand. John called me to the font, and I was prayed for and received the baptism. Was this being "born again"? Not in the sense of undergoing an emotional experience during which I suddenly found a great peace and joy in the arms of Jesus. I had always been a devout Christian; for me, my faith had been an ever-deepening belief rather than a revelation or conversion. Not as President Jimmy Carter had experienced his "very close, intimate, personal relationship with God through Christ" on a despairing day after he had lost the election for the governorship of Georgia. Not as Marabel Morgan had experienced her peace one day when, while shampooing a customer's hair in a beauty shop, she

173

suddenly found her peace. Rather, it was for me another phase of a constant growing love for Him.

Bob and I were divorced in the fall of 1972, fourteen months after he had left.

At nine in the morning, my attorney, Bill Nelson, an aunt, and I went to District Court on the fourth floor of the Coffeyville City Hall. We sat in hard-backed chairs in a chilly room. Voices tended to echo, so I judged the room to be barren and large. A light buzzing of sound told me there were only a handful of spectators.

Before we entered the courtroom, Bob and I and our attorneys had met briefly in the foyer and agreed to the conditions of the divorce decree. It stipulated that Bob would pay a regular sum for the support of the children; that I would receive the house, furniture, and the rest of the contents, and also the Village Shoppe with its inventory and fixtures. The provisions were read to me, and I agreed to them wordlessly. Bob was silent too.

Someone has said that a divorce is like a funeral because a marriage has died. At a funeral, there is love and fond memory of a human being who had gone on; in a divorce there isn't even that. There is only cold formality.

After about a half hour, the judge called my name, and I was led to a chair near the bench. He asked me to state my name, how many years I had been married, how many children I had by Bob, their names, their ages. The bleak, impersonal nature of the proceedings struck me forcefully, and I began to weep. Bill Nelson, intending to be helpful, told me he was handing me a glass of water. I reached for it, did not grasp it properly, and the water spilled over the pants suit I was wearing.

The judge read the conditions of the divorce decree, asked me if I understood them, and then said that, based upon our mutual agreement, the divorce would be granted on the grounds of incompatibility.

174

That was all.

Although our marriage has ended, Bob and I have maintained a friendly relationship, rather rare among divorced couples. He sees the children often, and they know they can count on him for emotional, not to mention financial, support.

Bob knows that he will be blamed by almost everyone —my family, friends, and society too. "That's understandable," he has told me, "and I can see it."

Bob has asked me not to "soften his image" in this story of my life, but to tell it as it happened. I reminded him that people who read it might think him a dreadful man, or worse, for having left a blind wife.

"I wouldn't doubt it," he said. "But this is real life, not fiction, and that was the way it was."

He was human and had reached his personal breaking point. Building a successful marriage is difficult enough for normal people; it is almost unimaginably hard when one partner is handicapped. Bob accepted the challenge and kept his commitment to "be my eyes" for many years.

If ultimately he failed, it was because the burden was too heavy and God never gives us any more load than we can bear.

Chapter Fifteen

In early April of 1974, Julia was wrestling with Pete, who was nearly three years old, on the sofa when one of her fingernails accidently scratched his eye. Whenever any of my children have even the most minor problems with their eyes, I tense up like a taut violin string. A young eye specialist had moved into town about two years before and had joined our church. I had met him once or twice briefly. I called for an appointment.

Next day, on a warm, fragrant morning, a friend drove me to his office.

It took the ophthalmologist, whom I will call Dr. Miller, only a few moments to determine that Pete had only a minor infection that could be cleared up with little difficulty.

Then he turned to me.

"When was the last time you had an eye examination?" he asked.

I thought back to my round of doctor-chasing, begun in pre-teens and ending when I was twenty-three. I was then thirty-eight. "About fifteen years," I said wearily. I told him what the final reports had been.

"I don't mind your looking at my eyes," I said, "but I know there's nothing you can do for me." I wish I had never said those words to that man. I hope he doesn't remember I said them! Still, I had been having headaches behind my eyes and knew that I should go. I made an appointment for the following day.

At 9:30 in the morning, the old familiar routine began

once more, beginning with a lengthy period of history-taking. Although this time, I could only hear and sense what was happening, I pictured it all vividly in my mind: the examination of the external portion of the eye and surrounding tissues, checking of the eyelids, the ophthalmoscope swinging before my eyes, the doctor peering through the powerful lenses as my chin rested in the support. He looked for a long time, examining the color and shape of the optic nerves, the blood vessels in and around them, the inner sides of the eye, the macula or the area in the retina which allows seeing persons to identify objects. He switched instruments turning to a slit-lamp microscope through which he examined the space between the cornea and the iris, and the iris itself.

In addition, I was given tests I had never had before. When I pointed this out, Dr. Miller laughed and said: "Fifteen years is a long time. We've learned much we never knew before and developed a number of new diagnostic and treatment techniques."

Finally, after five exhausting hours, he was finished. I heard him pull back his instruments. He asked me to go into his office.

"Charlotte," he told me, "the right eye is completely blind. There is no light perception whatever, and the eye has become shrunken and has lost its shape. But you do have light perception in the left eye with what we call good projection. That means you can tell from which direction the light is coming.

"Not only that but there is also what we call a good intopic phenomenon in the left eye, which means that you have a good color perception." He hastened to explain. "The eye has the ability to see its own blood vessel pattern."

I heard him writing at his desk. "Doctor," I asked, "do you have any suggestions for my right eye?" It had shrunk in its socket, and I had been thinking of having it removed and replaced with an artificial one.

The writing stopped. "I not only have suggestions for

that eye, but suggestions for the other one too. That was all he said, but in those few words was the hope I had never before heard in any doctor's office.

Dr. Miller asked me to wait in the outer office while he attended to some other patients. At 3:15, my friend Marilyn Lively dropped by to pick me up and drive me to a prayer group meeting which would start in fifteen minutes. "Well," she said, "are you ready to go? We . . ." She stopped suddenly, and there was a puzzled sound in her voice. "What is it, Charlotte?" she asked.

She had sensed a glow I was feeling which had radiated to my face. "I don't know, Marilyn," I told her truthfully. "I just don't know. But please go to the meeting without me because Dr. Miller wants to talk to me some more." She kissed me and she left. I sat there, my hands folded in my lap, waiting for Dr. Miller. I sat for more than an hour, and then he came out and talked to me.

"Now once it starts, uveitis cannot be cured," Dr. Miller said. "But it can be controlled. You see, years ago, when you developed your symptoms, the field of ophthalmology didn't understand the disease as it understands it now. We were still struggling to find the right medication to keep it under control. Today we have far more sophisticated drugs to keep the inflammation down and prevent it from destroying vision."

He told me that doctors still don't understand a great deal about why uveitus occurs, that it may arise from a number of causes. Viral infections, allergic reactions, and the spread of infections from somewhere else in the body have been cited as causes but never actually pinned down.

"About the right eye. One in ten blind eyes can harbor tumors, and pain can be the first sign. While there is no indication of a tumor at the present time, it must be watched carefully."

I nodded, waiting.

"But the left eye is a different story. The uveitis ap-

pears to be in a dormant stage. The iris—that's the pig-
mented area—has undergone a great deal of degeneration,
and a ripe, actually an overly ripe or hypermature, cataract
had formed over the lens." The lens, I knew, was a tiny
fluid-filled, oval-shaped part of the eye which is crucial for
proper vision. In order to see, light rays must pass unob-
structed through the pupil and the lens, which lies just
behind the iris. I remembered what Dr. Morse had told me
years before, that the lens is the eye's focusing mechanism.
With the help of tiny but powerful muscles, it thins out for
focusing on images that are far away and thickens for those
close by. From there the image is captured by the retina
and is transmitted by the optic nerve to the brain.

Normally, the lens is crystal clear. But for reasons doctors still don't understand, it can become cloudy or opaque,
usually, though not exclusively, in older persons. An opaque
lens, I had known since I was sixteen, is called a cataract.

I had known that one had formed over my left eye,
but Dr. Miller explained that because of the uveitis a mass
of dense, cord-like scar tissue had formed over and around
the cataract.

I asked pointblank: "Could an operation remove all
that scar tissue, and would it help me see?"

He was not certain. But he did tell me that he had
been trained in the military, and that in Vietnam he had
operated successfully on eyes that had developed thick scar
tissue from shrapnel, bullet wounds, and other kinds of
trauma. He told me about a Filipino woman, sightless for
many years because of uveitis, whose eyes had been almost
as bad as mine. He had operated, and her sight had been
restored.

"But I am not telling you this to rush you onto an
operating table," Dr. Miller said. "I cannot stress too
strongly that I am still not sure surgery is even possible in
your case. You see, we have to find out the condition of
the *back* of that eye, if the retina has been scarred or detached. Because of the density of the scars on the lens, I

cannot make that determination with the instruments I have."

Who could? During the years of my blindness, he explained, a diagnostic technique called ultrasonography, or tests made by sound waves, had been perfected. He explained that ultrasonography is a recently-developed medical tool utilizing sound waves that are pitched too high to be recognized by the normal ear. The vibration frequency range that we can hear, he said, ranges from 20 to about 17,000, but the human ear completely misses sounds that are above or below these figures.

"Because of the dense scarring," he pointed out, "I can't see with the instruments I have just what's there in back of your eye. But ultrasonography can. These silent vibrations are transmitted through your eye and then are bounced back onto an oscilloscope, which in turn creates a kind of picture graph of the tissues there. Doctors can detect abnormalities by comparing this 'sound picture' to ultrasonography in a normal eye. They can tell if any tissues have been lost or displaced.

"But even if the ultrasonography tests show no evidence of scarring or detachment, the odds against you are still very high," Dr. Miller warned me. "But let's take one step at a time."

Marilyn returned, and I left the office in a daze, clutching two names and addresses. One was that of a specialist in infectious and external eye diseases, the other a retinal expert who would perform the ultrasonography. Both were in Kansas City.

Events moved fast.

Two dear friends took Julia, Stephie, and me to Kansas City. On the way, I suddenly thought: This is Holy Week, the time of joy—and hope. Only a few weeks before, I had confided to some friends that I had just one wish, to be able to see for only three minutes. "I would use that time," I had said, "to look for one minute at each of my children's faces." *Was Jesus Christ, through a doctor, giving me that opportunity, and perhaps more, beginning on the week that celebrates His resurrection?*

Inside me, excitement was growing, but so many years had passed, so many other hopes gone glimmering, that I had to keep my expectations subdued. I cautioned my children, too, against building hopes which could, in a day or two, burst like soap bubbles. The time might not have arrived. Still, I couldn't keep them from chirruping like magpies all the way.

In Kansas City, the first doctor confirmed Dr. Miller's findings of a densely scarred membrane around the cataract. So far, so good. The big test was still to come.

Ultrasonography was as painless as Dr. Miller had promised. When it was finished, the doctor called us into his office, and I heard the sound of pictures being spread out.

"The retina," he said, "is pretty healthy under the circumstances."

I exhaled suddenly.

"This area right here," he went on, obviously pointing to a spot on a picture, "will be damned difficult in surgery."

So an operation might be possible, though Dr. Miller had to make the final decision.

Outside, I called Mother and told her to telephone Dr. Miller at once because I couldn't trust myself to speak. "Tell him what the doctor just told me," I pleaded. She did and called me back. "Dr. Miller is going to wait for the arrival of the reports, and then he wants to see you to discuss everything."

After he had received the reports, Dr. Miller called me in a number of times to perform countless other tests. He studied every part of the eye in minute detail, asked a thousand questions, made drawings on how he would approach the surgery.

Still he wanted me to be absolutely sure I wanted the operation. In the presence of my minister, Bill Nelson, he ticked off all the risks:

That the surgery would be extraordinarily difficult and

181

unusual. That even though the ultrasonograph showed no evidence of scarring or a retinal detachment, neither could be entirely ruled out. ("The positive graph is a good sign, but only means that abnormalities could not be detected.") That the thick, cord-like scarring over the lens meant that more blood vessels were there, greatly increasing the chances of a hemorrhage before or after the operation, and I'd lose the eye on the operating table. That an uncontrollable re-inflammation could occur, not uncommon after surgery, and again I would lose the eye.

"Charlotte," he summed up, "you could come out just being able to count fingers. You could come out being able to get around by yourself. You could come out being able to see the faces of your cihldren. Or you could come out the same or worse than you are now. I want you to go home and decide."

"I don't have to go home to make the decision," I answered. "I know. I want to have the surgery. I have no doubts about that."

But I had to wait. Dr. Miller's wife was about to have a baby. "I can't have her in the delivery room and you on the operating table at the same time," he laughed.

"I can wait," I said. "I waited for twenty years. A few more weeks won't matter."

Soon Dr. Miller's wife gave birth to a fine, healthy child, and we set the date for my operation.

On July 7, 1974, a hot Sunday, I entered the hospital, a pink stucco community institution on the edge of town, set back on a wide lawn. We walked through the small waiting room on the ground floor and into an elevator. I was led to Room 207, where I undressed and went to bed. Mother and the children remained with me much of that day. I wanted them to stay as long as they could because I didn't want to be alone with my thoughts. By now, it seemed the whole town knew, and the phone kept ringing constantly.

Finally, night came; a nurse gave me a pill, and I sank

into a deep sleep. In the morning, there was no time to start thinking again because the testing and pre-op prepping began. Mother and the girls were among my visitors and told me the whole town was praying for me.

Stephanie was at my bedside, reading to me, when the phone rang, it seemed for the hundredth time that day. It was Bob, calling from another state. Although the children had visited him often in the three years since he left and his support checks had arrived regularly, I had spoken to him infrequently during that time.

"Charlotte," he said, "I heard about the operation. I wanted to talk to you and wish you all the luck in the world. I am praying that the operation is a success because you deserve the very best."

I began crying and handed the phone to Stephie. He had not said he loved me or that he was coming home, but I believe that in his own way he was telling me he was sorry for all the hurt that terrible summer three years before. I can truly say that I was able to go into surgery with a forgiving heart, open to the Lord for His hand of healing through a young doctor.

That day, Dr. Miller came to my room.

"Are you an emotional person?" he asked.

I was surprised. "Yes," I admitted. "I cry when I'm happy and I cry when I'm sad."

"Charlotte," he said after a short pause. "When the operation is over, you must not cry." He repeated the injunction, this time underscoring each word: *"You must not cry."*

When I asked why, he explained that if I cried, I might squeeze my eyelids, and the wound, which would be sutured, might rupture. "Then everything done on the operating table will be undone," he said. "Don't ask anyone anything," he said as he left. "After the surgery, I'll come to see you and talk to you."

The last thing I remember saying to myself when I drifted off to sleep that last night was that I must not cry.

Chapter Sixteen

Tuesday morning. The anesthesiologist came to my room and asked me to extend my left arm. I felt a needle stab and, in a few seconds, I lost consciousness. Sometime afterward, I must have come out of this initial stage because I heard a voice in the operating room say: "Are you all right?" I remember replying: "I'm so cold." Anyone who has ever been through surgery will know that temperatures in operating rooms are always kept low. I was cold on the outside but felt warm and secure in the arms of God. Later, an orderly remarked to me: "I've been in a lot of ORs, but the atmosphere there, that morning, was somehow different. There was a kind of special calm there, and I think we all felt it." It *was* different, because in that room on that morning Jesus Christ was performing an act of healing through a doctor.

A few minutes after 8:00 A.M., I learned later from Dr. Miller, surgery was begun.

A six-foot-high operating microscope, which could magnify an area up to seven times, was wheeled to the table where I lay. Its swinging arm was centered above my left eye, and Dr. Miller peered through the twin eyepieces and adjusted the magnification the way he wanted it.

With instruments which are the most delicate used in any kind of surgery, he made an incision on the outer wall of the eye, under the upper eyelid where the white portion, or sclera, meets the dime-sized, dome-shaped cornea. Now he was in the eye's front chamber. The iris was the next structure he confronted, bound to the cataract by a thicket of scar tissue which had to be separated from it, tiny piece by tiny piece.

By 9:15, the iris had been freed from the cataractous lens. So far, so good. No hemorrhage has resulted. Next, Dr. Miller began the hardest part, removing the scarred, misshapen lens itself and creating an opening through which I could see. The problem he found was that scar tissue had pulled the cataract down from its usual position in the center of the eye. He severed the ligaments which hold the cataract in place from above, then formed a V-shaped opening in the lens to create a pupil through which light could enter. The difficulty was compounded by the fact that the lens tended to drop backward into the rear of the eye as he was trying to cut it loose.

Several times, Dr. Miller had to rest before proceeding.

10:45 A.M. By this time, the lens and all the scar tissue that had bound it to the eye was finally out. A new problem arose. After the lens was removed, the eye collapsed completely. Because of the extensive surgery that had been necessary, it had not maintained its round, spherical shape. He had to use special instruments to bring it back to its normal form.

11:30. The wound was closed with suture material finer than human hair, so gossamer-like that it seemed to float in the air even under the operating microscope. The doctor inspected the sutured wound, found it tight and leak-proof, so he knew the eye had been put back together. Then he examined the back of the eye with the microscope as best he could and found a good red reflex, which told him that the retina was still firmly in place and that there had been no bleeding.

The eye was medicated and bandaged, and the operation ended four hours after it began.

I was taken to the recovery room. An hour later, still heavily sedated, I was returned to my room.

Tuesday night. When I awoke, Dr. Miller's instructions not to ask anyone anything had slipped out of my mind. My first words to the nurse were: "Is everything all right?" She answered: "Charlotte, everything came out all right. Go back to sleep." Of course, that told me nothing about the restoration of my sight. When I awoke again, Dr. Miller was at the bedside. "It went fine," he told me, but even he could not tell yet. I slept some more.

Wednesday. In the morning Dr. Miller returned to my room and began removing the bandages, layer by layer. I lay with my eyes closed.

"Charlotte," Dr. Miller said. "Open your eyes and look up here."

I did and saw brightness, a sheet of light, more than I had ever seen in years.

"Now Charlotte," the doctor said. "I'm going to put a magnifying lens in front of your eye to take the place of the lens we took out. It lets your eye bring images into focus." He leaned over me.

"I'm holding up some fingers, and I want you to try counting them."

I looked toward the light, and some shapeless blobs were waving before me. I counted slowly. "One. Two. Three."

"Very good," Dr. Miller said. "Now can you tell me what this is?"

I saw a mass of color, like a fuzzy abstract painting. Slowly, the magnifying lens brought it into focus. I recognized it.

"A rose," I said. "It's a red rose." He had snipped it from one of the bouquets in the room and was holding it in front of my eye.

He replaced the bandages. I heard him say, "That was right. Now go back to sleep."

Still groggy from the sedation, my mind was unable to grasp the monumental meaning of what had just happened.

186

I needed round-the-clock care because the slightest jarring could open the wound and wreck everything. My friends and family knew I could not afford professional help, so they drew up a roster of volunteers who took turns sitting with me every hour of every day. Marilyn Lively was in charge of the schedule, and she ran things like a top sergeant, passing along Dr. Miller's injunctions to each one: "She must keep her head as still as possible. If she wants something, get it quickly. If she wants to talk, listen but don't prolong the conversation. She should talk as little as possible."

Everyone who was scheduled came on time; most ahead of time. They sat and they prayed. Marilyn told me later that all the volunteers were people who were deep in the walk with Jesus.

Thursday. The nurse came in and gave me an injection that sent me spinning. I've never been drunk before, but I thought: "Well, this must be the way it feels." I wondered why I was given this extra sedation, but I didn't have to wait long.

In a daze, I heard Dr. Miller's voice. "Charlotte," he said. "I don't want you to be upset, but Julia's had a little accident. She broke her kneecap and is down in emergency right now. But she's going to be fine." Well, whatever they had given me made me feel fine too, so I just said: "Okay," rolled over, and went back to sleep.

Julia, I learned afterward, had taken a ride on a friend's minibike and promptly collided with a tree on the family's broad backyard, breaking her kneecap in three places. She was taken to a room directly below mine where she celebrated her fourteenth birthday.

She and a few friends were stuffing themselves with birthday cake and pizza while I lay upstairs, sleeping it off. Apparently, Julia wasn't overly concerned about her own surgery which was scheduled for the next day.

It went well, and Julia was taken down to her room.

187

Saturday. Dr. Miller unwrapped my bandages again, cleaned the eye, and separated the lids. He told me the wound looked intact and that the eye chamber was normally formed. Then he put on my eyes a pair of temporary cataract glasses with extra thick lenses.

My eyes were closed when he put the glasses on. He told me to open them.

I saw a human face for the first time in fifteen years.

"I'm glad my doctor is a handsome man," I said.

"That's only because you haven't seen anyone for so long."

"Are you wearing a tie with polka dots?" I asked.

"I sure am.

"Let's see if you can read," the doctor said, and handed me a card with letters and numbers of different sizes. I held the card close to my eye and looked at it hard for several seconds.

"The first number is an eight," I said.

There were two nurses in the room. Although I hadn't moved my head to look, I knew they were there by the sound of their feet. I heard one of them sob.

"That's correct," Dr. Miller said. Reaching down, he took off my glasses. Then he said, not severely: "It's strange. We send our nurses to school and teach them all the facts about caring for patients, but we never can do a thing with their emotions."

I wanted to see my children, but Dr. Miller said it was too early. He was afraid the excitement would prove too much, that somehow my head would be jarred, injuring the wound. Most of all, he was afraid of my tears.

Sunday. A big scare. In the examining room across the hall, Dr. Miller saw something wrong. A film had appeared over the iris. He told me that this was a fairly common occurrence following surgery and that it can disappear.

"But suppose it doesn't?" I asked. "Suppose it grows and makes me blind again. How long will I have to see?"

He was frank. "I'm not sure. *If* it grows, it depends on

how fast. I'll return tonight, and we'll be able to know more."

Disappointed? Yes, but frightened? No. I had been through too much adversity to be frightened. Maybe this was not yet the time.

"If it is growing, Doctor," I said, "I want to see my children."

In the evening the doctor returned, wheeled me himself to the examining room, and peered closely into my eye. "Charlotte," he said at last. "I think we can breathe safely. The wound is still in the healing stage, and I don't think it will grow." It never did.

The following Tuesday, a week after the operation. Dr. Miller came in and said: "Today you're going to learn to walk again by yourself."

For years I had clung to someone, or Polly had guided me. Reading my thoughts, Dr. Miller said: "And you're not going to hang on to anyone."

I got out of bed and walked to the door. The corridor was about 100 feet long, and the nurses had pushed away everything I could possibly bump into. Wearing my temporary cataract glasses, I began my walk, followed by a nurse and Dr. Miller. I walked steadily for about twenty feet, then was told to turn and come back. My nurse wanted to know: "Now Charlotte, just how much of this can you really see and how much are you doing by some kind of hidden radar?"

Each day and night after that I walked a little farther until I could go all the way to the end of the corridor and back.

Wednesday morning. I saw Stephie for the first time since she was an infant. She was now fifteen years old.

By this time, the heavy bandages had been replaced with a protective shield. It was removed, and the temporary cataract glasses were put on my eyes. A very bright light was brought near the bed.

Stephanie walked into the room and stood at the foot

189

of the bed. I gasped. She looked exactly like a youthful Grandma Johnson, whose luminous face in church so many years ago had made me determine to give my life to Jesus.

I looked at Stephie's light-colored hair which covered her forehead in the style of the mid-70s and said: "Stephie, we're just going to have to do something about those bangs." She grinned and brushed her hair back, and I could see her beautiful peaches and cream complexion, those large, wonderful eyes, and warm, wide smile. My firstborn.

Wednesday afternoon. I saw Julie for the first time.

She was still in the hospital, recovering from her knee-cap surgery, and I had to go to her. I put on a gaily colored housecoat and, my tension mounting, walked down the corridor and into the elevator. Two nurses and Dr. Miller were with me.

Julia's door was open. A lamp had been turned so it shone fully on her bright pink face with its soft brown hair brushed off the high forehead. Someone had told her about Stephie and the bangs. I stepped inside and stood at the foot of the bed, looking at my daughter. Now two more nurses from the floor had entered and were standing in the doorway. Julia smiled at me, and then her eyes began to glisten.

Later, I learned that tears were rolling down the nurses' faces as they watched. Dr. Miller's eyes, too, were filling up, Dr. Miller who the week before had spoken with mock-severity about nurses who do not learn in school to control their emotions.

Of them all, I was the only one who remained dry-eyed, though my heart was pounding and my lips moving. I was not allowed to cry.

Ten days later. I had recuperated to the point where Dr. Miller felt I could see Pete. But, he cautioned, he must not be allowed to jump on me in his excitement. Pete was only three.

I told Mother that there was a little outfit that I wanted

him to wear and to put that on him. By this time Julia was out of the hospital. Stephanie was in summer school, so Julia and a friend brought Pete up. Julia was on crutches. I was lying on my bed. There were nurses, and Bill was there too.

I was looking at the door, and there he appeared, a little boy in a white short jump suit with a navy blue shirt, navy blue knee socks, and white sandals. He was so very still and stiff; his little arms were very close to his sides as he walked over to the bed and said, "Hi, Momma." He hardly moved.

I cupped his little face in my hands, the little baby face. I'd never seen my girls when they were babies that age, and this was the first time I had seen him. I seemed to drink in all those years of babyhood with all three of my children in one little boy's face. He had huge brown eyes and a darling little face. He stood there for at least fifteen minutes. He didn't move a muscle, and let me look at him. Nobody said a word.

Then Pete said, "Momma, I want to show you something. This is my elbow and Momma, this is my shoe, and Momma, this is my ear. Here's my back. And here's my knee, Momma. Here's my ankle." And he showed me every part of his body. It was quite an experience for a three-year-old boy, to show his momma everything. He went around the room in great excitement and brought me everything. He brought me books. He said, "Momma, did you see this? Somebody gave you this, Momma. Here are these flowers, Momma." He was going a mile a minute. It was like something had been unleashed inside of him, something he had to control before because his momma was blind and he knew his momma was different. Now his momma was like any other momma and she could see, and he was going to show her everything.

He left and I was exhausted after that experience. I kissed him and Julia good-by and went out into the hall.

The elevator hadn't come yet, and my friend and Pete and Julia were standing there. Pete turned around, saw me, and ran back toward me with his arms out. I couldn't stoop over, but he put his arms around my knees and hugged me good-by again and said he loved me.

Chapter Seventeen

It was time to go home. Mother brought some clothes, and I dressed for the first time in almost a month. I'd lost a lot of weight, so I looked like a little girl wearing her mother's dress. "Drive carefully and don't hit any bumps," the doctor warned Mother as we left. That just about did it for her. In the car, she gripped the wheel and drove as though surrounded by eggs.

Before going home, she had a practice run—just across the broad street to Dr. Miller's office. We parked in the back, and I walked across the lobby. On my first venture into the outside world, even the vending machines against one wall fascinated me. I stood before them and stared. A few moments later I was in the office and seeing, for the first time, the place where my doctor worked and where I had made the decision to have the surgery.

I looked around the waiting room and stared at the chairs, the walls, the carpeted floor, then went into the treatment office. Dr. Miller looked at my eye a long time and finally said: "It looks good. It's healing properly, and the cornea is clearing up fine. Let's see how well you can read now."

He handed me a card containing a paragraph of type. The opening words were printed in large, bold letters, and the rest were scaled down gradually in size. I began reading and did not stop until I had finished. I had not seen printed words for twenty years, yet I had not forgotten. I glowed. Dr. Miller grinned as I gave him back the card.

Afterward, Mother drove home, slowly and carefully. "Thank heaven," she said aloud, "there aren't many cars on the street." I stared out, watching the homes and people walking past, remembering vividly that April morning, fifteen years and four months before, when Daddy was driving me to prayer after my sight went and I tried vainly to see anything, moving or standing, through the car window.

"That's where Joyce and Jim live," Mother said after a while. I saw my friend's home. Now my heart began thumping because I knew my own house was in the next block.

I looked to the right and there was the schoolyard I had "seen" so many times in my mind. Mother turned left into the driveway, and I saw a small white house with black trim and a red mat on the front porch. The door opened, and I could see three smiling faces greeting me. Pete was jumping all over. The girls couldn't contain him; he burst out the door, ran to the bottom step, and waited for me to get out of the car. As I approached, Pete's hand slipped into mine, and he helped me up the steps. The girls were holding the door open. "Welcome home, Momma," they said.

I walked into the living room. The sun shown through the gold drapes, the colors harmonizing with the gold, green, and brown of the sofa. I looked down at the gold shag carpeting. They hadn't had shag rugs in the 1950s, before I lost my sight, and although I had often touched the tightly woven loops, I was curious about the construction.

Pete insisted on an immediate tour of the rest of the house. Stephanie's room, decorated by her, was a very deep blue. She had a blue and green carpet on the floor and blue and green plaid drapes and bedspread. The walls were hung with psychedelic posters. I walked down the hall to Julia's room, lively and bright with an orange shag carpet and two shades of orange paint on the walls. Pete's room had the white and gold furniture that we'd used for the girls. On his bed were heaped Sesame Street and Winnie the Pooh toys.

By this time I was ready for my bedroom and rest. I had to stay in bed for about three months, in and out, and toward the end, I was more out than in bed. I couldn't have visitors at first, but the local newspaper printed an article telling how I was getting along. Friends and neighbors brought our food in for about a week, and Mother took her vacation that first week I was home so she could help me.

A few days later, my high school class had its twentieth reunion. I wasn't able to go, nor indeed could I have visitors yet; but that day a huge plastic pillow arrived signed by every member of the class who was still anywhere near town. That day, another surprise. Dr. Miller had given Joyce permission to come to the house. From the bedroom, I heard her voice.

In a moment, she breezed in. "Hey there," she said, "how do you like the dress you picked out for me?" Before the operation, I had gone to market in Kansas City and selected dresses for the two of us to wear at the reunion. It was Joyce's way of saying hello, and it was just right for the moment. Anything more and the joy at seeing my best friend since second grade would have brought the tears I must not shed. I looked at her silently for a while, and we put our arms around each other.

Each day heaps of cards and letters arrived at the house, many from people I didn't know but who had read or heard about the surgery.

After several weeks, I was allowed to go downstairs for meals, and the very first time, I astounded poor Pete. From where I sat at the kitchen table, I could see right through the kitchen door into the utility room where the freezer was. Pete was at the freezer, getting an ice cream bar. It was right at supper time so I said, "Pete, you shouldn't be doing that." He put that ice cream bar back in the freezer and slammed the door and turned around. He put his hands on his hips and said, "Why, how did you know?" And then it dawned on him that I could see now, and a smile spread over his face. It was going to be a whole new world for three little kids, and a whole new world for one momma.

The world that had dawned only vaguely resembled the impressions I had had by feel and scent.

Rooms were much larger than I had imagined them. My own bedroom seemed vast. Hallways were longer. The loft where I had sung many years as a choir member towered higher than I had thought over the pews. And the sky. Its vastness utterly overwhelmed me.

Blind people live in a small box, with an area of existence extending only to where they can reach. Wherever I was, the end of my fingers was my world, and it had been impossible to visualize the enormity of what was beyond.

I found nobody, no human face unbeautiful, no shape or form or person unpleasing to the sight. I suppose a superficial explanation might be that, with my sight returned, I was so grateful that everything and everyone was beautiful, but I think the reasons are far deeper.

Because of the premium society puts on personal attractiveness, a seeing person unconsciously puts labels on people: they are pretty, ugly, fat, handsome. These judgments usually stick and color your attitudes toward them. But I couldn't see, so I had to use other standards. Because I couldn't see what a person looked like, I got to know them from the inside, where true beauty lives. Now that I can really see, appearance is meaningless. I don't really see the outside of a person at all; my concentration is within.

In a way, I can thank God for my blindness because I learned to see correctly. I find beauty in the ordinary things about me, the petals of a rose, the shine of the chrome sink faucets, the texture of a hand. On one of my first walks alone in the hospital, I came upon a beautifully grained wooden door at the end of the corridor. Each day I could see it clearer, and I would stand there, touching it, marveling at the rich distinctive figures worked into the wood. I had never before even looked at a door, much less admired the spirals and waves in one.

One day we had potatoes baked in aluminum foil. I took it off and absent-mindedly began wadding it up as I had always done. Then I looked at it and gasped out loud. The inner folds glinted and sparkled like cut diamonds. I sat looking at it, entranced. Crushed ice in the bottom of a red plastic glass caught the light and gleamed like rare rubies.

A sidewalk—an ordinary cement walk on which people step every day of their lives. Who notices it? I saw its varying shades of gray, the jagged cracks where the cement had broken, the pearly stones at the edges of the squares where the cement had worn away. The grass along its borders was a deep cool green but—another revelation—it was no longer a solid block as it had been in the days when I could see. Each blade now rose up from the soil, its own independent self. I could sit and study grass for an hour.

Wordsworth wrote:

> To me the meanest flower that blows can give
> Thoughts that do often lie too deep for tears.

Emerging from blindness, I learned anew the nature of the Creation in which we humans spend each day of our lives. It is far more lovely, more varied, more complex, and more beautiful than most of us, busy with day-to-day living, ever realize. All this beauty is there, open to everyone who has eyes to see.

I had never been able to read to any of my children. Now Pete, a curious, inquisitive child, would come home from school (actually a preschool program) and tug at my sleeve, book in hand, "Come on, Mom, it's time for us to read."

His favorite book was *Thank You God—for the World in Which We Live*. He would cuddle into a chair beside me and listen quietly as I read the story to him again and again.

At last Dr. Miller gave me permission to leave the house, coupled with warnings that I must be "very careful and not overdo." He said I could go to church and even go down to the store. He added some more cautions—no lifting, no sudden movements, and only a few hours a day at the outset.

I was a little apprehensive about seeing the store. Bob had designed it—it had been his dream for many years and had become mine as well. I forced myself to go. A tiny bell tinkled as I opened the front door, seeing for the first time the shake shingles forming a roof over the hanging racks, the beautiful wood fireplace, the comfortable furniture scattered about, creating a warm, homey atmosphere.

How beautiful it is, I thought, and then, almost inevitably, how sorry I was he hadn't waited; that his timetable was not the Lord's timetable.

I didn't dwell on that too much, however, but plunged once again into my world of store, community, and, most importantly, family.

We would take long rides into the surrounding countryside to observe the changing seasons. Several times the girls and I went to Tulsa where I window-shopped for hours until they pulled me away.

Once Julia and I even flew to New York City for a three-day visit. I had been there shortly before Bob and I were married, and I pointed out the sights to her. Both of us were fascinated with the busyness of it, the crowds moving through the streets, the stores filled with gorgeous things, the movies and theaters with glittering productions.

One day, Pete's teacher invited the parents to school where she showed films she had taken of the children while they were working and playing. She did this every year and, in the past, Pete had sat beside me and whispered what was happening on the screen. There was a look of pure joy on his face this time as we sat and watched the film together.

The store was not doing well financially. An urban renewal program had torn up streets and sidewalks in the area months before, and customers found it difficult to park or get to us. My financial backers conferred with their accountant and decided to sell the store. I was not unhappy at the prospect because I had begun to resent the long hours and endless planning that go into the retail business. I wanted to be able to spend that time with my children.

Plans were made to sell off the merchandise and close up the next month. Shortly before that, Pete and I were browsing in the town's music shop. The owner and I had a delightful conversation and she offered me a part-time job which I happily accepted.

My days and nights were filled with job, church choir, occasional bridge games, and meetings with old friends, many dating back to the days when Bob and I were a couple. Stephanie and Julia were performing in *Godspell*, and I was asked to do the vocal coaching. Another time Stephanie and Pete had roles in *Carousel*, and I helped out on that too. When you have active children, you have to be an active mother, and I threw myself wholeheartedly into their activities.

About this time, Dr. Miller advised me to give Polly away, which saddened me a great deal. Polly had been with me for two and a half years, had given me much independence, and I had grown very fond of her. However, she was trained to be a leader dog, to exert a strong pull on the person holding the harness and, following my surgery, I could not be jerked or pulled. I gave Polly back so that she could, once again, be somebody's eyes.

A few months after my surgery, Coffeyville residents produced a musical show to raise money for the town hospital. I was grateful to the hospital auxiliary, which was sponsoring the show, because it had donated the equipment used in my operation and, when they asked me to take a part, I agreed immediately.

The show was called the "Pink Garter Follies of 1974," and I appeared in the finale. When I walked onstage, wearing a long white and silver gown, I had a broad smile on my face. But inwardly, I was trembling. How to explain to this audience how I felt, my joy, my gratitude that I could be there, alone, unaided on that stage!

The auditorium at Field Kindley was packed, but there wasn't a sound to be heard. Many in the audience knew me, had been with me in spirit throughout my blindness, and I could feel their love and encouragement.

I began to sing, "Let there be peace on Earth and let it begin with me." I can truthfully say that I felt every person in that auditorium was singing with me. They were with me in my joy.

Mother and I had decided to look for a house together. She was always helping me do things, watching out for Pete, chaperoning the girls. We were always over at her house, or she was at ours, and we all got along real well, so it seemed to be a great idea.

One day we rode past an old, rambling house with a bay window and huge porch. It was so much like one that kept recurring in my dreams, dreams from which I awakened with a feeling of peace and contentment, that I was sure the Lord had taken us to it. I set out immediately to see if it was for sale. It was, and we bought it and moved in a week before Christmas.

To increase my income I decided to look for a full-time job and made applications at several places without any luck. I began to feel that employers were hesitant about hiring me because of my sight, so I went to see Dr. Miller.

"They're used to seeing me totally blind," I said dismally. "They look at me now, and I know they wonder if I can really see well enough to do the job." I was very discouraged.

Dr. Miller didn't say a word, reached out for his telephone, and called Dean Daniel, the president of the First National Bank where I had just applied for a job. The president had a booming voice and, with my acute hearing, I heard his words.

"You know, Dr. Miller, we were just going to call you. We wanted to know if you thought Charlotte could handle this teller's job." Dr. Miller assured Mr. Daniel that I could.

So now I work in a bank. I run the machines, I type, enter deposits, count out money, and, at the close of day, I balance my window to the penny. Each morning I leave my home at 7:45, walk down the broad, tree-shaded streets to the granite-faced bank; and at the end of the day, I walk back home. It has been several years, but the thrill of being able to do just that has not left me, nor will it ever.

I try, in some small way, to repay the Lord for helping me regain my sight by comforting others who have problems with their eyes. Often I am asked to speak at meetings for the blind or those with impaired vision. While I cannot, of course, hold out hope for a miracle like mine, I do urge them to have faith, never to give up, and to keep useful and active.

I have gone privately to visit persons I have heard about, to encourage and, in some cases, to give practical advice on coping with daily tasks. Many organizations for the blind have programs to teach blind people how to manage, of course, but I feel that a personal home visit from somebody who has been there does a lot for the morale.

In May of 1977, I sat in the high school gym and watched Stephanie, in gray cap and gown, receive her diploma. The following year I saw Julie walk to the platform and accept hers.

I will be there many times more in the coming years to see school activities, and then I'll come again in the late 1980s. That's when Pete will graduate, and I will see that too.

I am certain that a miracle had restored my sight, not the kind of spectacular, instantaneous cure one generally looks upon as a miraculous occurrence, but genuine nonetheless. It was Jesus who led me to a doctor in my small city, a doctor who had had special experience with my own very rare eye problem. It was Jesus who brought me to him, and it was Jesus who guided his hands as he opened the world to me once more.

Epilogue

Ever since the doctor had warned me about crying, I had kept a tight rein on my emotions. I held back tears, whatever happened.

On a winter's day six months after the surgery, I was alone in the house, looking out the window. The lawn was covered with a new blanket of snow, white and smooth. The old oak that shaded us in summer was naked of leaves now, and I could see the hard blue sky through its jutting branches.

I cannot remember what triggered it. Perhaps nothing at all happened. But suddenly, at long last, the tears came, great tears that flooded my face, tears of joy, of gratitude to everyone who helped and of thankfulness to God for the miracle that had allowed me to see His handiwork again.